5

Middlemarch
from Notebook to Novel

Middlemarch
from Notebook to Novel

A Study of
George Eliot's Creative Method

JEROME BEATY

+ //

ILLINOIS STUDIES IN LANGUAGE AND LITERATURE: *Vol. 47*

THE UNIVERSITY OF ILLINOIS PRESS
URBANA, 1960

Board of Editors: HARRIS F. FLETCHER, JOHN R. FREY, AND JOSEPH R. SMILEY.

To

Laurel and Shawn

Foreword

This is a study of George Eliot's composition of *Middlemarch* based on her letters and journals, the notebook she kept while writing the novel, the *Middlemarch* manuscript, and the corrected proof of the first (parts) and so-called Cheap (1874) editions of the book. It proceeds more or less chronologically from the author's first mention of a projected novel to be called "Middlemarch" on January 1, 1869, to her completion of the "Finale" on October 2, 1872. Each portion of the novel is treated according to the chief compositional problem it involves. The first eighteen chapters of *Middlemarch* are a fusion of the beginnings of two separate prose works; chapter 1 of this study attempts to reconstruct the original beginnings and the rewriting and new writing that fused them. George Eliot rearranged the next fifteen chapters of *Middlemarch* to accommodate the novel to the experimental form in which it was to be published (half-volume serial parts); chapter 2 of this study analyzes these changes and the over-all influence of publication in parts on the novel. About the time she began chapter 34, George Eliot started making extensive use of her notebook to plan the rest of her novel; chapter 3 of this study traces these plans and changes of plan through the notebook to the resultant portions of *Middlemarch*. Of course throughout her writing of the novel George Eliot was making innumerable choices and changes which can now be traced only through the revisions she made in the manuscript; since it is impractical, however, to attempt to analyze the thousands of changes in the 1,200-page manuscript, chapter 4 of this study examines in detail the revisions in one more or less typical chapter, chapter 81.

Chapter 81 is not merely any typical chapter in the *Middlemarch* manuscript, however. According to John Cross, George Eliot specifically described how she wrote the chapter and stated that this was her usual creative method when she was doing her best work. Her description, though hitherto often quoted by critics of her novels, is clearly and incontestably contradicted by the number and nature of the revisions in chapter 81. Analysis of these revisions thus offers a new and different version of George Eliot's creative process from that now generally accepted.

This new description of George Eliot's creative process may not alter our evaluation of her novels. Indeed, my purpose is to separate, if possible, discussion of the creative process from criticism of a work and to force a re-examination of such pseudocritical terms as "spontaneous," "contrived," "unconscious," and "conscious" in order to divest them of some of their equivocal meanings—they can refer either to the creative act or to the aesthetic effect, and a demonstration of one is not necessarily proof of the other. It was not to answer the question, "Is *Middlemarch* a great novel?" but, "How did George Eliot write that great novel *Middlemarch*?" that this study was undertaken.

My debts are many. Without the generous grant of a traveling fellowship for the year 1951-52 by the Graduate College of the University of Illinois, the research in London and Edinburgh on which this study is largely dependent would have been impossible. I particularly wish to thank Mrs. Helen Hay of that office for her assistance.

This book is based on my University of Illinois doctoral dissertation, "*Middlemarch* from Notebook to Novel: A Study of George Eliot's Creative Method" (Urbana, 1956). Professor Royal Alfred Gettmann, whose encouragement, advice, assistance, and friendship were so essential to the completion of that work, has, as friend and adviser, helped me see the material into this form. The fellowship gave me the means to begin, Professor Gettmann the means to complete this book.

No scholarly work on George Eliot could be completed without frequent recourse to Professor Gordon Sherman Haight's vast knowledge of her life and work. In addition to answering my many queries, he kindly sent me proof sheets of pertinent portions of the text of his edition of *The George Eliot Letters* before their publication. I am deeply grateful to the staff of the British Museum and, in particular, to Mr. Arthur Jefferies Collins, until 1955 Keeper of Manuscripts, and Mr. Alfred Henry Spiller of the Department of Manuscripts for their friendly assistance. The Librarian, Mr. William Beattie, and the Keeper of Manuscripts, Mr. William Park, of the National Library of Scotland were most kind and helpful in making available to me the Blackwood correspondence with George Eliot and George Henry Lewes before the publication of much of this correspondence in the Haight edition. Though I used the letters in manuscript, I have adhered here to the readings in the Haight edition, just as I have converted references from the Cross *Life* to that edition. I wish to thank Wing Commander George Douglas Blackwood for making accessible to me the corrected proofs of *Middlemarch*. I am indebted to Mr. Alexander Dallas Wainwright, Curator of the Morris L. Parrish Collection in the Princeton University Library, for his assistance. I am indebted also to the Research Committee, Graduate College, University of Washington, for its generous grant. To Mrs.

Margaret Graybeal and Miss Esther Erford I owe thanks for their cheerful tirelessness in typing this material. Finally, I thank my wife and son for their patience and cooperation while I spent so many hours rightfully theirs on this work. Though my debts are to many, whatever faults and inadequacies this study may have are owing to no one but me.

Chapter 4 of this work appeared in somewhat different form and with somewhat different emphasis in *PMLA*, 72 (September, 1957), 662-79, under the title, " Visions and Revisions: Chapter lxxxi of *Middlemarch*."

Contents

Middlemarch
from Notebook to Novel

CHAPTER ONE

"Middlemarch" and "Miss Brooke"

About New Year's Day, 1869, George Eliot set herself the task of writing a novel to be called "Middlemarch,"[1] but it was not the novel we know by that title which she foresaw. Though she was planning a novel of provincial life,[2] like the novel we know, and though one of the chief characters—she thought of him then as the hero—was a physician,[3] that earlier "Middlemarch" was without Dorothea, without Casaubon, without Will Ladislaw.

George Eliot began writing this earlier "Middlemarch" about July 19, 1869,[4] and by September 11 she had completed an introduction and three chapters.[5] She reports no further specific progress, though from September, 1869, to the end of May, 1870, she occasionally worked on the novel. On May 23, 1870, it was still much in her thoughts, and she spoke of her intentions regarding it at some length with her publisher, John Blackwood, though she had to admit she was "not so far [along] as she intended to be."

For five months we have no word about "Middlemarch." About the beginning of November, George Eliot began another story, describing it in her journal on December 2, 1870: "I am experimenting in a story which I began without any very serious intention of carrying it out lengthily. It is a subject which has been recorded among my possible themes ever since I began to write fiction, but will probably take new shapes in the development. I am today at p. 44." In the remaining four weeks of 1870 she added another fifty or more pages to the new story, which had by then been given the provisional title, "Miss Brooke." George Eliot never again mentioned "Miss Brooke" as a separate work. When, on March 19, 1871, she wrote in her journal "my Novel," she

---

[1] Gordon S. Haight (ed.), *The George Eliot Letters* (7 vols., New Haven, 1954-55), 5: 3—hereafter cited as *Letters*; where date of letter appears in text I give no volume or page reference since the edition is arranged chronologically.

I put the title of the earlier "Middlemarch" in quotes and italicize the title of the published novel *Middlemarch*.

[2] *Letters* 5: 99.

[3] J. W. Cross, *George Eliot's Life as Related in her Letters and Journals* (3 vols., Edinburgh and London, 1885), 3: 100—hereafter cited as *Life*.

[4] *Life* 3: 95.

[5] Cross omitted the sentence reporting this progress from *Life*. Professor Haight kindly called this to my attention but did not include the journal entry in *Letters*.

undoubtedly referred to the new *Middlemarch* made up at the time of the beginning of the earlier "Middlemarch" and all or most of what she had written of the once-separate "Miss Brooke."

The history of the composition of the first several hundred pages of *Middlemarch* is thus largely the history of how the separate beginnings of "Middlemarch" and "Miss Brooke" were joined, a story which, to my knowledge, no one has hitherto tried to reconstruct, though the fact of the two beginnings has been evident since the publication of Cross's *Life* in 1885 and every reader of *Middlemarch* who has read that *Life* must have wondered about the details of the fusion.[6] Only George Eliot herself could have completely, conclusively, and authoritatively satisfied this curiosity, but she did not choose to do so. A careful study of her journals, her notebook, and the corrected manuscript of the novel,[7] however, answers some of the questions of the curious completely, some partially, some not at all, and it permits a reconstruction of the fusion of the two works which, however partial and, in places, conjectural, is as close as we can hope to get to the true and complete story. Such a reconstruction this chapter attempts.

Both the published and unpublished entries in George Eliot's journals from this period are useful only in establishing the fact that *Middlemarch* originated from the beginnings of two separate works and in reporting roughly what progress had been made on each. They give no direct indication of when or how the fusion was achieved. Nor is the notebook George Eliot kept while writing *Middlemarch* much more helpful. Only the manuscript in the British Museum offers evidence—evidence, not answers to our questions. This evidence consists of the differences in paper stocks that George Eliot used, the spacing of her writing, and

---

[6] Professor Haight has called to my attention a list of "Questions about the original MS of Middlemarch" found among Lord Acton's papers but not in his hand:

"Did fusion take place between Jan. 1 and March or between March and July?

"How many pages of Miss Brooke were written before the plan of fusion was adopted? To what point in the story?

"At what point in the narrative was the Middlemarch narrative dropped previous to the death of Mr. Lewes' son?

"Was a part of Chapter XI as it now stands written in to effect the fusion?

"Was Chapter XV 'introductory' or did it stand after Chapter XIV in the original MS?"

It is evident, especially from the last two questions, that the questioner had given considerable thought to the problems involved in reconstructing the fusion and was thoroughly familiar with the novel, though perhaps not with the manuscript. There are no answers to these questions among the papers. I had posed and attempted to answer these same questions (but not, directly, the third) independently, before they were brought to my attention.

[7] For descriptions of the *Middlemarch* notebook and manuscript see p. 133, "Descriptions of Primary Sources."

certain key changes she made. She used two stocks of paper in this part of the manuscript: one is watermarked " Parkins & Gotto " and is unlined (see Illustration 1, Appendix A) ; the other is watermarked " T & [J]H 1869 " and contains twenty-three ruled lines to the page (see Illustration 3, Appendix A). On some of the lined pages George Eliot wrote only on the ruled lines; on others she semispaced, i.e., wrote about forty-five lines to the page. " Middlemarch " names appear in " Miss Brooke " chapters and vice versa; these sometimes have had to be inserted as revisions in the original text. In addition, in two separated passages, but only in these passages, Mary Garth was surnamed at first " Dove " and revision was necessary. Certain evidence that one would expect to find if these pages were original drafts of the openings of two separate works, e.g., sequences of renumbered pages, is missing, but even without such evidence definite conclusions could be reached if all the extant evidence pointed in the same direction. As we shall see, however, it does not always do so.

Certain points, nevertheless, may be established with relative certainty: by March 19, 1871, George Eliot had written the first eighteen chapters and what is now chapter 23 of *Middlemarch* and had already joined the two separate beginnings.

The journal entry for that date states, " I have written about 236 pages (print) of my Novel, which I want to get off my hands by next November. My present fear is that I have too much matter, too many ' *momenti.*' " Despite the parenthetical interpolation, it is manuscript, not printed pages, to which George Eliot referred. At that time she did not even know in what format her novel was to be published; an estimate would thus be impossible. Even if she were to judge on the basis of the page length of her earlier works, it is extremely unlikely that she could hazard so close an estimate as precisely " 236 "—not " 235 " or " 240," but " 236 ": the handwriting in the earlier portions of the *Middlemarch* manuscript is so uneven, the spacing so disparate in " Middlemarch " as well as in " Miss Brooke " portions, that much later even George Henry Lewes had to ask the publisher to set up type samplings of the differently spaced and written pages " in order to form a calculation of quantity " ; [8] surely, then, whatever the format, George Eliot herself could not have calculated how many printed pages her manuscript would make. Moreover, chapter 23 (which was at this time still considered chapter 19) ended, before certain late revisions, on a page George Eliot herself had numbered " 236," [9] and the end of a chapter is a good stopping place

[8] *Letters* 5: 185.
[9] The *Middlemarch* notebook, published by Anna Theresa Kitchel as *George Eliot's*

and reference point for reporting progress. It seems relatively certain, then, that the reference to 236 pages is to manuscript pages in the present joined version of *Middlemarch*; the parenthetical " print," I believe, is simply George Eliot's way of indicating that the pages were fully packed ones, each on the average equal to a page of print in the usual format.

With chapter 18, in which Mr. Brooke appears in an otherwise essentially " Middlemarch " chapter (involving the vote on the chaplaincy of the new hospital) , the two separate stories become more and more closely interrelated. It is with this chapter also that the first notebook entry clearly having to do with the joined *Middlemarch* deals. A list of directors of the new hospital headed " Middlemarch " on *Quarry II*, 2, includes Dorothea's uncle, " Arthur Brooke Esq. of Tipton Grange," and this list is followed on the same page by a sketchy map which tries to fuse such " Miss Brooke " places as Tipton into the " Middlemarch " area, and on the next page by a list of " Relations to be developed," including " Caleb Garth to Mr. Brooke etc." and " Mr. Farebrother to all, except Sir J. & Mr. Brooke," which is as close as the notebook comes to showing George Eliot trying to join the two stories. The implication of these notes is clear: chapter 18 is either the first chapter to be written in its entirety after the fusion of the two works or, at least, is the first such chapter to join elements from both " Middlemarch " and " Miss Brooke." This is consistent with the supposition that by March 19, 1871, George Eliot had gone a chapter beyond that point, had by then joined what she had had of " Miss Brooke " and " Middlemarch " and was preparing to launch herself into the writing of the new *Middlemarch*.

Other indications point in the same direction. George Eliot's fear of too many " momenti " suggests that the two plots, each with its own incidents, had been put together. So does the manuscript; in its earlier portions, repagination, revisions, differences in the spacing of the writing and the stocks of paper all suggest that two separate stories were being joined, but after chapter 18 or chapter 23 there is no such evidence. Further, there is nothing to indicate that " Middlemarch," which had been virtually abandoned at the end of the third chapter more than a year and a half earlier, could have reached its two hundred and thirty-sixth page in March, 1871, nor is there anything to indicate that " Miss Brooke " ever got beyond the end of its tenth chapter (now the middle of chapter 10) , at which point it begins to merge into *Middlemarch*, for the next " Miss Brooke " chapters (19-22) , though their sequence

Quarry for " Middlemarch " (Los Angeles, 1950) , also indicates (p. 47) that the then chapter 19 ended with page 236. Following Miss Kitchel's designations (see p. 133, " Descriptions of Primary Sources ") , I henceforth cite the notebook as *Quarry I* or *Quarry II* and use George Eliot's pagination; the editorial matter I cite as Kitchel.

has been changed within the new novel, show no signs of having been rewritten or repaginated from " Miss Brooke " originals. The few indications there are, then, and the absence of expected evidence to the contrary, strongly imply that the March 19 journal entry refers to about nineteen chapters of the joined *Middlemarch.*

It is within these 236 pages, then, that whatever evidence there is of how the two stories became *Middlemarch* lies. The first ninety-six of these pages, nine and one-half chapters, deal exclusively with the " Miss Brooke " story. Are these pages in the British Museum manuscript of *Middlemarch* in fact the pages of the very draft that George Eliot meant to be the beginning of a separate story called " Miss Brooke " ?

There is no evidence that these pages were rewritten or recopied to any significant extent; there are two pieces of evidence which indicate that they were not. First, the journal entry of December 2, 1870, indicates that George Eliot was at page 44 on that day. In the British Museum manuscript, page 44 ends chapter 4. Since the end of a chapter is a good stopping place and point of reference, the manuscript referred to and the one in the British Museum would seem to be one and the same. Second, and far more conclusive, is the fact that the only name from the " Middlemarch " portion of the novel which appears in these chapters—and it is the name of the town and district of Middlemarch itself—necessitates a revision in the manuscript on each of its five appearances in this part (four times in chapter 6, once in chapter 8) , i. e., it is inserted and an original word or phrase is deleted. On its first three appearances it refers to the district, and the original reads, " the county . . ." ; the last two (?) words unfortunately are illegible. Most of the material deleted on the fourth appearance of this name is completely obliterated, but the name itself in chapter 8 is partially legible—it seems to be something like " Misterton." " Middlemarch " appears for the first time without having to be inserted in the manuscript on the very first page (p. 97) of the dinner-party scene in chapter 10 in which the Vincys, Bulstrode, and Lydgate—" Middlemarch " characters—appear, at which point in the novel the two stories obviously have already been joined.

George Eliot did not find it necessary to recopy or rewrite " Miss Brooke " in order to join it to the long-stalled " Middlemarch." This much we can establish. But can we establish how much of " Miss Brooke " was written as a separate work? That is, did she get as far as this tenth chapter with the separate " Miss Brooke," or, conversely, did she get beyond this point and discard the additional pages when the two works were joined?

The length of the separate " Miss Brooke " can be established only within certain limits of probability. The external evidence of the December 31, 1870, journal entry is itself not precise, although it helps fix the limits. George Eliot wrote, on that last day of 1870: " I have written only 100 pages—good printed pages—of a story which I began about the opening of November, and at present mean to call ' Miss Brooke.' "

It is not known how soon after this entry George Eliot began to join the stories, though, from the number of pages completed by March 19, 1871, and the obvious amount of rewriting and new writing that must have been done before 236 pages of " my novel " could have been completed, it appears certain that the author began to work on the new *Middlemarch* very soon after this entry. Even assuming this to be the exact point at which *Middlemarch* was conceived, we have difficulty translating the estimate of " 100 pages—good printed pages—" into terms of manuscript pages. If this were, in fact, an attempt by George Eliot to estimate the length of what she had written in terms of printed pages, we do not know with what format in mind or on what basis she was estimating. But with completion of the work, and even the negotiations for publication so far off, would George Eliot attempt an accurate estimate? It would seem improbable. On the bases of this improbability and of the adjective " good " (why " *good* printed pages " ?) we may conclude that this was not an attempt to estimate the printed length of the manuscript at all, but that it was simply a description of the pages, like the " 236 pages (print) " of her March 19, 1871, entry, i. e., George Eliot had written about one hundred manuscript pages, not skimpy ones, not twenty-three lines to the page, but full ones, each about equal to an average printed page. If we can with safety make this assumption, and if we can assume that " Miss Brooke " was abandoned as a separate work soon after this entry, we can say that it apparently reached the end of the then chapter 10, since the " Miss Brooke " portion of the beginning of *Middlemarch* ends with manuscript page 96 in the middle of the present chapter 10.

The manuscript evidence in some small measure confirms this assumption. Since it was necessary to insert the name " Middlemarch " in the text and delete some other name as late as the next to last page in chapter 8, we can be sure that " Miss Brooke " reached at least that point as a separate work. It is possible that the dinner party in chapter 10 which introduces " Middlemarch " characters appeared in " Miss Brooke " in some other form, but it is also possible that there was no dinner-party scene at all. The fact that there is to be such a party is introduced rather abruptly, at the end of a mild argument between Dorothea and Mr. Casaubon, on page 96 of the manuscript (1: 130),[10] but, if this page was

---

[10] References to the printed text of *Middlemarch* are to the Cabinet Edition (3 vols., Edinburgh and London, [1878]) unless otherwise specified.

part of " Miss Brooke " and the dinner-party scene has simply been rewritten, there is even stronger evidence that " Miss Brooke " reached at least this point. Page 97 begins, " Sometimes when Dorothea was in company, there seemed to be as complete an air of repose about her as if she had been a picture of Santa Barbara looking out from her tower . . . (1: 131) ," completing the last fully " Miss Brooke " paragraph before the introduction of " Middlemarch " characters; but at the bottom of page 96, after " the entire absence from her manner and expression of all search after mere effect," five full lines and some writing in the margin have been deleted. These lines are for the most part illegible and seem to have been themselves revised before the deletion, but their gist appears to be a contrast between the effort to seem and Dorothea's inner ideal standard. These revisions and deletions may simply indicate that George Eliot had trouble with this sentence, but, coming as they do before the first " Middlemarch " page, they may indicate that the present page 96 was at one time joined to another, more strictly " Miss Brooke " page 97.

The indications of the journal and the manuscript, though neither is in itself conclusive, when combined, strongly suggest that the first ninety-six or ninety-seven manuscript pages of *Middlemarch*, nine and one-half chapters, are the original draft of what was intended as the beginning of " Miss Brooke." Little, if any, that was written as part of that separate story had to be discarded, perhaps only the last page or two of its tenth chapter. These chapters brought " Miss Brooke " up to Dorothea's departure on her honeymoon and perhaps represented the major portion of George Eliot's original conception of that story. Why, then, did George Eliot come to recognize " Miss Brooke " and " Middlemarch " as possibly parts of one novel at this point?

To the reader of the finished novel the similarity between the careers of Lydgate and Dorothea is obvious. Both have high ideals which come to nothing or little more than nothing; in both cases an unwise and unhappy marriage plays a part in obstructing the realization of these ideals. That this is the theme of the Dorothea story, with the added implication that for a woman in nineteenth-century England the only possible way of realizing these ideals was through marriage, is clear in the " Prelude " and in that part of the " Miss Brooke " story we know was written before it was joined to " Middlemarch." We cannot be sure, however, that this theme was part of the author's original conception of " Middlemarch." It is possible, then, but not certain, that the two separate works were joined when it became apparent to the author that their themes were similar.

The time element and scene in the two stories are similar, if not identical. Though this similarity may not háve caused the two stories to be joined, it did little to prevent it. The time of the actions is more obviously similar in the two stories than is the scene. " Miss Brooke " takes place before the first Reform Bill when provincial families were " still discussing Mr. Peel's late conduct on the Catholic question " (1: 10) ; the year is specified in the " Middlemarch " portion of the novel as 1829, and there is evidence in the early pages of *Quarry I* that George Eliot was reading up on medical conditions and practices in 1830 for the background of the original " Middlemarch." Though most of the events of " Miss Brooke " take place in the rural districts and most of the " Middlemarch " events in the town itself, their complementary nature as part of provincial life, perhaps even specifically Midland life, offers little difficulty to seeing them as part of the same book.

If the similarity of theme in the two stories " triggered " setting off the idea of joining the two stories, and if the similarity of the time element and scene caused no difficulty, there still remains the question of how George Eliot was primed to see them as one. Perhaps no such priming was necessary; perhaps the idea of uniting the stories came to her in a flash of inspiration. But perhaps there was priming.

In the first nine chapters of " Miss Brooke " three plot lines are being prepared: the course of Dorothea's apparently doomed marriage to Casaubon; Mr. Brooke's standing for Parliament; and Will Ladislaw's growing relationship to both the marriage and the campaign. If at this point George Eliot still had no intention, as she herself had said when she began the story, of " carrying it out lengthily," there would seem to be too much plot material. The introduction of matter other than that directly related to the course of Dorothea's marriage to Casaubon, i. e., of the Mr. Brooke and Ladislaw material, would thus indicate a change in the original plan of a rather short story, perhaps a short novel. But since it is clear that all of these chapters were written as part of " Miss Brooke " and not as part of the joined *Middlemarch*, it was not the joining that caused the change in plans. What was it then?

George Eliot, on December 2, 1870, said she " *began* [" Miss Brooke "] without any very serious intention of carrying it out lengthily " (italics mine) , as if the doubt whether this was true even on December 2 had occurred to her. She warned that it " will probably take new shapes in the development." On that day she was at page 44, the end of chapter 4. Up to that point in the story the possibility of Mr. Brooke's standing for Parliament has not been mentioned; he " goes into things," collects documents, etc., but until chapter 6 does not seem to have ambitions for a seat in Parliament.[11] Will Ladislaw neither appears nor is mentioned

[11] The possibility of Brooke's stand is first mentioned by Mrs. Cadwallader, who

in these first chapters. He is mentioned first, indirectly, in chapter 8, and he appears for the first time in chapter 9. Thus sometime between December 2, 1870, when George Eliot had completed four chapters of " Miss Brooke," and December 31, when she had completed about one hundred " good printed pages," her original intention not to carry out " Miss Brooke " lengthily had been abandoned, for by the latter date enough plot material had been introduced to bear a tale of some length, certainly too much for a very short story.[12]

Then, on or about December 31, she reached the end of the first major plot line: Dorothea was married to Casaubon and off on her wedding journey. The author was about to plunge into a full-length, perhaps even three-decker length, story. But this was the end of the year when it was George Eliot's habit to tot up her accomplishments. There was the beginning of " Middlemarch," long abandoned. To interrupt it for a poem or for even a longish short story was one thing; to continue " Miss Brooke " to novel length was another. The air was primed for the sudden flash of insight which would recognize the two stories as part of one great novel of provincial life in the last years before the first Reform Bill.

Between the day of decision, December 31, 1870, or soon thereafter, and March 19, 1871, when George Eliot had completed 236 pages of the now joined *Middlemarch*, lay innumerable possibilities and consequently innumerable small decisions, a vast amount of rethinking and replanning, some rewriting, and some new writing in order to make the two separate stories fuse smoothly. There lies for us, consequently, a vast amount of surmising, assuming, deducing, and reconstructing. For it is our present purpose to discover, between pages 97 and 236 of the manuscript of *Middlemarch*, whatever has remained of the original fifty or more pages of " Middlemarch " and to reconstruct as far as possible the steps George Eliot took in fusing the beginning of " Middlemarch " and the beginning of " Miss Brooke " into the beginning of the new *Middlemarch*.

appears here as a minor character for the first time. Her name now appears in chapter 1 but had to be added to the original text; her name in both chapters 4 and 5 has been changed from an original which in the latter instance at least seems to have been " Mrs. Lydgate "!

[12] Cf. Gerald Bullett, *George Eliot* (London, 1947), p. 216: " In these [first] ten chapters [of *Middlemarch*] . . . George Eliot excelled herself . . .; for here we have not only the authentic George Eliot . . . but something that we have too often felt the lack of in her work hitherto: an ease of manner, . . . an all but effortless mastery of her material. . . . Whether this new grace is the effect of her having no ' very serious intention ' of writing the story lengthily, one can only conjecture; but the difference in tone . . . is unmistakable."

Not only does this border on equivocation—the not very serious intent and the not very serious tone (" ease of manner ") confusing the tone of the work with the method of composition—but Mr. Bullett applies the December 2 journal entry to chapters (5 ff.) which were written later.

Few suppositions and little reconstruction are necessary in identifying the first subsection, pages 97-112. These pages were written after George Eliot decided to join " Miss Brooke " to " Middlemarch " ; they serve as a bridge from the " Miss Brooke " chapters which precede them to the " Middlemarch " pages which succeed them. There is no contradictory evidence; there is a great deal of confirming evidence. All of these pages, like those of the preceding " Miss Brooke " chapters and unlike almost all the rest of the pages in the four volumes of manuscript are Parkins and Gotto paper. Characters and the names of places and characters from the two separate works mingle freely and without revision on most of these pages. Even Mary Garth's name appears without revision.

Nevertheless there are subgroups of pages whose origin is less certain than that of most of the rest of the group. We have already seen that the manuscript evidence does not conclusively identify the origin of the dinner-party scene in chapter 10 (pp. 97-102) , though it does suggest—as does the useful nature of this scene in introducing " Middlemarch " characters into a " Miss Brooke " chapter—that the chapter was written to help join the separate works. Very definitely the present draft of the scene postdates the fusion of the two stories since characters from both sources mingle freely without revision of their names in the manuscript.[13] The first four pages of chapter 11, pages 103-6 (to " This was the case one morning of the October in which we have lately seen Mr. Casaubon visiting the Grange " [1: 145]) , constitute a bridge between the two earlier stories even in conception: they are largely taken up with describing Lydgate's preference for Rosamond over Dorothea; " Miss Brooke " names appear in this " Middlemarch " section without revision. The last pages of chapter 11 (pp. 107-11) seem to belong to the same draft, but, since no names from " Miss Brooke " appear, there is no positive proof. There are three indications, however, that these pages should be so identified. First, like the other pages in this section and unlike pages 113 ff., they are Parkins and Gotto paper. Second, the presentation of Rosamond's character, through her deliberate scheming to meet Lydgate, when considered with certain other indications in this portion of the manuscript suggests a later development. Finally, Mary Garth is mentioned six times on pages 109-10, and only on the first appearance was her surname changed from " Dove," [14] a clear indication that these pages were written after the

---

[13] The lawyer's name, " Standish," was here changed from " Shaw." It appears in chapter 14 (1: 200) without revision. This would appear to be as much an attempt to economize on the number of characters as to join the characters from the two stories.

[14] The name " Garth " may have been written first, " Dove " over it, and " Garth " over " Dove." Either George Eliot decided to use " Garth " at this point or wrote " Dove " from force of habit.

subsequent " Dove" pages (114-19 and 146-52) . Though this draft of the scene surely belongs to the bridge period, the scene itself may have been conceived as part of the original " Middlemarch." The first distinctly " Middlemarch " scene in the manuscript—the " Dove " section, perhaps part of the first chapter of the original—opens in the middle of the young Vincys' approach to Stone Court; something obviously preceded it introducing Fred and Rosamond to the reader, and if it is not certain that it was the breakfast scene, neither is there reason to believe it was not. Pages 107-11, then, are in the present draft part of the bridge between " Miss Brooke " and " Middlemarch," but they may have been based on an earlier draft, perhaps the opening pages of the latter story. The first page of chapter 12 (p. 112) may be similarly identified. Something must have preceded page 113, but it probably was not page 112: page 113, like the " Dove " pages that follow it, is " 1869 " paper and page 112, like the bridge pages that precede it, is Parkins and Gotto paper. On this Parkins and Gotto page, " Lowick," a " Miss Brooke " place-name, appears twice without revision. Page 112 is clearly part of the bridge draft, and page 113, though it does not contain Mary Garth's surname, seems part of the " Dove " draft.

The first sixteen pages of manuscript after the end of " Miss Brooke " have been established, then, with relative ease and relative certainty as bridge pages, written after the decision to join " Miss Brooke " to " Middlemarch," with the last six of these pages identified as possibly a redraft of an early portion of the original " Middlemarch." In the next one hundred or more pages (pp. 113-236) lies what remains of the " Introduction," the rest of the first chapter, the second and third chapters, and whatever else was written of that earlier beginning of *Middlemarch*—at least forty manuscript pages.

With page 113, from Fred's saying to Rosamond, " ' They are, though. That is Mrs. Waule's gig ' " (1: 156) , begins a jungle of evidence and counterevidence of how the two stories were joined. On some pages there are no traces, on some many traces, and on others contradictory traces of their origin. These evidences and traces identify, sometimes definitely, sometimes not so definitely, certain groups of manuscript pages as belonging together. There are, for example, " Dove " pages, on which Mary is so surnamed, and there are semispaced pages on which George Eliot has written forty-five or so lines, two to each ruled line on the page. These pages will be discussed in apparently homogeneous groups, though at times other pages will be brought in to clarify certain situations. It will be well to remember throughout that not all evidence of rewriting, shifting, etc. is necessarily evidence of a " Middlemarch " origin; much rewriting and replanning was done, apparently, on material that had not been written before the fusion of the two stories took place.

Before we examine these pages section by section, we must make one thing clear: the two major sources of physical evidence, paper and pagination, indicate, superficially but unequivocally, that *not one page* of the original draft of the earlier "Middlemarch" remains (with only two possible but not clear exceptions). All of the first 112 pages of manuscript are Parkins and Gotto paper; except for the first two pages of chapter 15, none of the rest of the manuscript of *Middlemarch* appears on this paper. The Parkins and Gotto pages were written in November and December of 1870 (as part of "Miss Brooke") and during part of the period from January 1 to March 19, 1871 (as part of the bridge). The " T & [J]H 1869 " paper was used from page 113 of the first volume throughout that volume and throughout the second volume, most of which was written after March 19, 1871. The " 1869 " paper stock thus seems to have been used later than the Parkins and Gotto. Since all of the " Middlemarch " scenes are written on this later paper, it is obvious that none could have been written when we know " Middlemarch " was written, in the summer of 1869. All of the 1869 draft, then, according to the testimony of the watermarks, must have been recopied or rewritten into the new *Middlemarch.*

This is the same conclusion to which the pagination points. If some of the pages subsequent to page 113 were written as part of the old " Middlemarch " there would surely be some trace of the early page numbers. There are a few deleted page numbers in this part of the manuscript but none in such long sequences or so low—on the order of 1-50— as to suggest that the pages so renumbered formed part of the original opening of " Middlemarch," the only portion of the earlier story we know for certain was written. The combined weight of the evidence of the paper and the pagination seems to prove conclusively that *none* of " Middlemarch " remains, in its original draft at least, in the British Museum manuscript of *Middlemarch.*

The evidence of the paper stock alone would not be conclusive. The first part of *Felix Holt* is on paper watermarked " Couper's Extra Super," but even in the first volume of the manuscript the Parkins and Gotto paper found in *Middlemarch* was also used.[15] The entire manuscript of *The Spanish Gypsy,*[16] written after *Felix Holt* but before *Middlemarch,* is on paper other than Parkins and Gotto, watermarked with an elaborate

---

[15] B.M. Add. MSS. 34,030-32. No Parkins and Gotto paper appears in the second or third volume, although " Couper's," a crown watermarked paper like that used in *The Spanish Gypsy,* " P & [JG]," and unwatermarked paper do appear.

[16] B. M. Add. MSS. 34,033.

crown design. The basic paper for the first two volumes of *Daniel Deronda*, the novel which followed *Middlemarch*, is watermarked " Alexr Pirie & Sons," but in the first volume there are two pages on " T & [J]H 1869 " paper, which had not been used extensively since the first eighty pages of the third volume of *Middlemarch*, and two other pages on " T & [J]H Kent," which was the basic paper for the latter half of the third volume and all of the fourth volume of *Middlemarch*; furthermore, after "Towgood's Extra Super" became the basic paper for *Daniel Deronda* in the second half of the third volume, about 125 of the 300 pages of the fourth volume were written on " Pirie " paper.[17]

With such evidence that George Eliot frequently had more than one stock of paper on hand at any one time—paper was, by Victorian times, after all, rather inexpensive—and used them almost haphazardly, it would be difficult to make a case for the time of composition of any one section of any of George Eliot's novels on the basis of the paper alone. Since Parkins and Gotto paper was used in the early portions of *Felix Holt*, a possibility suggests itself that the newer " 1869 " paper may have been used earlier than the older Parkins and Gotto stock: George Eliot, at first not intending to write " Miss Brooke " at length, may have used what was left of an old stock of paper—Parkins and Gotto—though she was using " 1869 " paper, of which she had a good supply on hand, for " Middlemarch," which she did intend to write at length, presumably in the usual three-decker format; when she came to join the two novels she used up her stock of Parkins and Gotto paper on the bridge pages, and, still using some of the " Middlemarch " draft, continued on with " 1869 " paper.

The lack of significant repagination is more difficult to explain away. Some possible explanations are: (1) that the earlier page numbers were trimmed away when the manuscript was bound—some of the page numbers in the " Miss Brooke " section were trimmed away, but no considerable consecutive run of pages was so trimmed; (2) that the earlier page numbers happened to coincide with the last two digits of the present numbers, e. g., page 113 was page 13 in " Middlemarch " and only a " 1 " had to be prefixed—but there is no evidence of this in the color of the ink; (3) that the pages in the earlier " Middlemarch " were not numbered—this is contrary to George Eliot's usual practice and, though Cross does not quote them, twice page numbers are mentioned in the journal (August 29, " At p. 40 of Middlemarch " and September 11, " At p. 50 ") and though these are round numbers, they are references to page numbers; (4) some of the page numbers which have been changed (e. g.,

[17] B.M. Add. MSS. 34,039-42.

pp. 140-45, 146-54, 169-70, which seem to have been changed from 145-50, 173-79, and 171-72, respectively) were really changed from " Middlemarch " page numbers somewhere between 1 and 50 but the older numbers can no longer be detected. None of these conjectures is convincing, but one of them, or some similarly remote possibility, may just happen to be true. The absence of repagination strongly suggests, but does not prove incontrovertibly, that practically nothing of the original draft of " Middlemarch " remains in the British Museum manuscript.

Although the physical evidence of the paper and pagination points clearly to the conclusion that almost nothing of the original draft of the " Middlemarch " manuscript remains, certain internal evidence points just as clearly in the opposite direction. It indicates, for example, that pages 113-19 and the opening pages of chapter 14 (MS. 1: 146-54) were written very early. They were certainly written before the bridge pages and probably before the decision to join " Middlemarch " to " Miss Brooke." They appear to be first drafts, however, not copies of pages written earlier; in other words, they seem to be part of the original draft of " Middlemarch."

But let us look more closely at this internal evidence, homogeneous section by homogeneous section where possible, disregarding for the time the physical evidence.

The first section is not clearly defined. It begins with page 113, but it may end either with page 119 or with page 124. It is a " Dove " section. It continues on from the bottom of the last Parkins and Gotto page [18] with the approach of the young Vincys to Stone Court. Inside, before Fred and Rosamond enter, Mrs. Waule, Peter Featherstone's sister, is telling her brother that Bulstrode, another of Fred's uncles, has accused the young man of paying off gambling debts with promissory notes based on Fred's expecting to inherit old Featherstone's property. The young Vincys enter; Mrs. Waule leaves. Page 119 ends with Mary and Rosamond about to leave the room to let Featherstone speak to Fred: " ' Come into my room, Rosamond, you will not mind the cold for a little while,' said Mary. The two girls had not only known each other in childhood. . . . Indeed " (1: 163) .

In these seven pages Featherstone's Christian name appears three times. Only the first time (MS. 1: 118 [1: 161]) was it necessary to delete "⟨Jacob⟩" and insert " Peter "; on the very next page and thereafter throughout the novel it is " Peter " without revision. This is the kind of change one would expect to find only in a first draft, though it is not conclusive proof that these pages are in fact a first draft.

---

[18] Page 112. The writing toward the bottom of this bridge page seems spread out to meet an already-written page 113.

On MS. 1: 116 (1: 159), Mrs. Waule speaks to Mr. Featherstone of his
"heart complaint." A note very early in *Quarry I*, undoubtedly made
early in the "Middlemarch" period (latter part of 1869), long before
George Eliot even thought of writing "Miss Brooke," much less of joining
it to "Middlemarch," also shows her interest in heart disease. The notebook and novel both suggest, then, that Lydgate was to treat Featherstone
for heart disease. But there is now no other indication in the later chapters dealing with Featherstone's illness that he is suffering from heart
trouble; instead, it is Mr. Casaubon who is stricken with and dies of
"fatty degeneration of the heart." Mr. Casaubon's affliction does not
manifest itself until chapter 28, which George Eliot wrote after she had
joined the two works, indeed, after March 19, 1871; she did not delete
"heart" from the phrase "heart complaint" on MS. 1: 116 until she
corrected proof. Attributing heart trouble to Peter Featherstone was
clearly left over from a "Middlemarch" intention, before Casaubon was
part of the novel, though not necessarily conclusive evidence that page
116 was written in the "Middlemarch" period.

In these pages only one "Miss Brooke" name appears, "Lowick"
(MS. 1: 119[1: 162]), and it was inserted, the original, illegible except for
an initial "B," [19] having been deleted. This is better evidence of the
"Middlemarch" origin of these pages, though because of its single occurrence it is not conclusive: George Eliot may have first written the
"Middlemarch" name because of her unfamiliarity with the new *Middlemarch* landscape.

Finally, there is the surname "Dove" given in these pages to Mary
Garth. This could hardly have been due to an oversight, for the name
had appeared seven times in these seven pages and had all seven times
been "Dove." George Eliot then deleted all seven appearances of the
name, five times replacing it with "Garth," and twice merely omitting
Mary's surname from the passage.

Whether the next five pages (pp. 120-24) belong to the preceding
"Dove" section or the succeeding "Garth" section is not certain, since
neither Mary's surname nor any "Miss Brooke" name appears therein.
The revisions at the bottom of page 119 and the top of page 120 might
indicate that the author had joined the pages from different drafts, but
they were more likely due to her difficulty in presenting Rosamond's
character, a difficulty which necessitated much revision in the early portions of the manuscript. That there are relatively few revisions on pages

[19] Mr. Farebrother's church is St. Botolph's. His name, when it first appears in the
manuscript, was changed from "B⟨u⟩rrow." These facts and the later relationship
between Mary and him perhaps indicate that it was in his parish that Featherstone
lived in "Middlemarch."

120-23 suggests that George Eliot might have been basing these pages on an earlier draft, but the number and extent of revisions vary so greatly from page to page and chapter to chapter that it is difficult on the basis of the number of changes to draw conclusions about the origin of so small a section as this one. Whether or not these pages are part of the " Dove " draft, some version of them is presupposed by that draft, for the matter on pages 113-19, especially Mrs. Waule's talk with her brother, prepares for the subject matter of these pages, Mr. Featherstone's demand that Fred get a testimonial from Bulstrode to the effect that the banker does not believe Fred is borrowing money on his prospects of inheriting Stone Court. The second " Dove " section (pp. 146-54) presupposes this request since it is concerned with Fred's delivery of the note from Bulstrode.

This later " Dove " section contains all of the second Fred-Featherstone dialogue—in which Fred produces the note from Bulstrode and is rewarded with one hundred pounds—and the first two and one-half pages of his six and one-half page conversation with Mary (to " ' You ought to have a little fellow-feeling there, Mary,' " 1: 208) . Between the first " Dove " section and this one Mary's surname appears twice as " Garth " without revision. On these pages it is first " Dove " on all four appearances, three of which George Eliot revised and one which she deleted. This would seem evidence enough for identifying the two passages as portions of the same draft and of a draft other than that in which the name " Garth " appears without revision. These nine pages name no " Miss Brooke " person or place, so there is no evidence of revision or lack of it to introduce, but there is slight evidence that this may be a first draft: John Waule's Christian name has twice been revised from the earlier " Thomas."

The appearance of " Dove " in both these sections identifies them as parts of the same draft and dates their composition earlier than that of the bridge section and that of the intervening " Garth " section. The change of proper names seems to indicate a first draft. The necessity for revising the name of the parish to conform to the " Miss Brooke " name, " Lowick," used in the bridge section, and for eliminating the identification of Featherstone's ailment as heart trouble, point to a " Middlemarch " origin for these pages. As in the case of the evidence of paper and pagination which indicated that there were no remaining " Middlemarch " pages, this evidence, which clearly indicates that these pages are " Middlemarch " originals, can be explained away piece by piece, but its cumulative force is all but conclusive. The " explainings-away " are conjectural, even improbable, but since the two " probable " conclusions are flatly contradictory and irreconcilable, each becomes itself " improbable."

Without arbitrarily dismissing the internal evidence, it is impossible to date these pages later than the bridge section. We are left, then, with the alternative of accepting them as original " Middlemarch " pages or as a " true copy " of " Middlemarch " pages made after the join but before the writing of the bridge section.[20] These " Dove " sections shall, then, be treated as part of the original " Middlemarch," though, in this area of improbabilities, this cannot be demonstrated with certainty. If anything of the original manuscript of " Middlemarch " exists in the British Museum manuscript of *Middlemarch* (except, perhaps, the last two pages of chapter 15) it is these " Dove " pages which begin chapters 12 and 14. If they are not in fact originals, they certainly belong to the older conception of the novel and, in any attempt to trace the merger of " Middlemarch " with " Miss Brooke," may be treated as originals.

The two " Dove " passages comprise the beginnings of chapters 12 and 14. Between the two are several small sections of manuscript. In the first of these (pp. 125-30) George Eliot followed the ruled lines and used the surname " Garth " twice. In the second small section (pp. 131-34) concluding chapter 12, she also used this surname, but here she semispaced, writing two lines to each ruled line, the first such spacing in the manuscript. She also semispaced the first half (pp. 134-38) but not the latter half (pp. 139-45) of chapter 13 and renumbered all but the first of these regularly spaced pages in this chapter.

Though we should now concentrate our attention on the pages which intervene between the two " Dove " passages, the second of the passages contains a deleted series of numbers, apparently 173-79,[21] which forces us to extend our examination of this portion at least up to page 180, i.e., to include all of chapter 15 (pp. 160-70) and at least the beginning of chapter 16.

Though not all of the pages from the middle of chapter 12 to the

[20] So to date them and yet claim they are new rather than a recopying is psychologically and materially unsound. Even by March 19, George Eliot feared she had " too much matter—too many *momenti*," and indeed her novel soon outgrew even the three-decker format; yet the Fred-Mary plot line, though important, is certainly the least essential in the novel, and it is extremely unlikely that it would appear in the new *Middlemarch* if it had not already been part of the old, especially since it does little to link " Middlemarch " to " Miss Brooke." Why would George Eliot, upon realizing that " Miss Brooke " and " Middlemarch " could form parts of the same novel, begin not with a linking passage, not with one of the main story lines, but with that portion of the novel neither common to both nor central to the new novel? Besides, when she first started " Middlemarch " in September, 1869, her journal indicates that she began the " Vincy and Featherstone " parts.

[21] There is a 173 and a 173a; the last digit of the number of the page following 177 and the entire number on the next page are illegible; presumably these were pages 177a and 178 or 178 and 178a. At least one digit of all these deleted page numbers is illegible.

middle of chapter 16 are semispaced, discussion of those semispaced pages within that section necessarily involves that entire portion of the manuscript. Since such pages occur only here in the four volumes of the *Middlemarch* manuscript, it may be assumed that this spacing may have something to do either with the original " Middlemarch " or with the blending of that work with " Miss Brooke," and that an examination of these pages may reveal not only their origin and function but help explain such factors as the appearance of " Garth " unrevised on pages 125-30, the revised pagination of pp. 140-45 and 146-54, and the peculiar pagination of the first part of chapter 16, as well as other characteristics of and changes in these pages.

Why are these pages, and only these pages, semispaced? Before this question can be answered, certain points, some of which are even more important than the general question, must be cleared up: Are these pages part of the original draft of " Middlemarch " or are they a redraft of the original " Middlemarch " pages? At what period of composition were these pages written or rewritten (if, indeed, they are part of a homogeneous draft) ? If, like the " Dove " pages, they are part of the original " Middlemarch," why are they not written in regularly spaced lines as are the " Dove " pages? If, on the other hand, they are part of the bridge passage or other " Garth " passages, why are their lines also not regularly spaced? Does the conclusion or conjecture which explains the semispacing of the lines also explain some or all of the other characteristics of these and surrounding pages?

First, then, are these semispaced pages part of the original draft of " Middlemarch " ? Some of the material in the first of the semispaced sections (pp. 131-34) at the end of chapter 12 would certainly seem to belong to the original " Middlemarch." This section begins with Mary's hearing Featherstone ringing the bell: " ' is the bell—I think we must go down ' " (1: 173) . He rang the bell on page 125, the intervening pages containing the Mary-Rosamond conversation which took place simultaneously with the Fred-Featherstone conversation of pages 120 ff. (It is important to remember that these two conversations could have been written as parts of different drafts.) The girls join Fred and Peter Featherstone; Rosamond, *delaying until Lydgate can arrive*, sings two songs for old Featherstone; the *planned-for* meeting with Lydgate occurs and their flirtation begins; the young Vincys leave for home, Rosamond thinking of Lydgate and Fred thinking of the unpleasant duty of getting the note Featherstone demanded he get from Bulstrode and planning to ask his father to make the request for him. This last has been prepared for by the Fred-Featherstone conversation and itself prepares for the Mr. Vincy-Bulstrode conversation in chapter 13 and thus for the second Fred-

Featherstone conversation in the " Dove " passage in chapter 14 (so that this semispaced section could not have been written earlier than the " Dove " sections unless the latter were recopied) . Unlike the other semi-spaced sections, this one contains elements of the Fred-Featherstone third of the plot complication of this part of the novel. The meeting between Lydgate and Rosamond also seems to be part of the original " Middle-march " (otherwise there would be no reason for her presence at Stone Court) , though it is possible that the details surrounding this meeting were not the same in the original. This scene, then, was probably part of the original " Middlemarch," but these pages do not seem to be the original draft. They are not part of the " Dove " draft because unlike that draft they are semispaced. They were composed later than that draft, perhaps later than the bridge section which contains a " Dove " to " Garth " revision, because on the very first page of this section the name " Garth " appears without revision (1: 174) , the only appearance of Mary's surname on a semispaced page. Probably later than the " Dove " sections, certainly later than the bridge section, these pages as they now stand postdate the joining of the two stories.

The second semispaced section (pp. 134-38) opens chapter 13. It presents Mr. Vincy's determination to call on Bulstrode, the Lydgate-Bulstrode conversation which delays Vincy's interview, Vincy's inter-ruption of that conversation, and his inviting Lydgate to dinner. It carries the action up to the point of Vincy's conversation with Bulstrode about Fred, i. e., to " ' The fact is, it's about a whim of old Featherstone's. Somebody has been ' " (1: 192) .

That these pages are semispaced and pages 140-45 are not strongly sug-gests that they are not of the same draft. If this is the case, the semispaced pages seem to have been written later than the regularly spaced ones. On the last of the semispaced pages the lines are more open, as if being spaced to meet a predetermined point, a conclusion hinted at if not con-firmed by page 139, which, while not semispaced, seems to belong with the former group of pages, for not only is it, like them, not renumbered, but several times on that page the author wrote or began to write two lines per ruled line. It looks as if pages 138 and 139 were spaced to meet a page that had already been written. Further, since pages 135-38 contain references to Mr. Vincy and on these pages he is even for a time present, they could not have been written before the second half of the chapter was at least conceived; but the Vincy-Bulstrode conversation on pages 140-45 contains no reference to Lydgate or his interview, so these pages might have been written independently of that interview. Also, the Vincy-Bulstrode conversation forms a link between the two " Dove " passages in the story line involving Featherstone's demand that Fred get a testimonial from Bulstrode. Therefore, according to our tentative identification of those " Dove " passages, this interview belongs to the first three chapters of " Middlemarch," completed before September 11, 1869. But pages 135-38 contain the seeds of the chaplaincy dispute, a plot situation which evidently postdates the writing of chapter 3 of " Middlemarch." An entry in *Quarry II* which deals chiefly with the duties of the house surgeon and chaplain is headed " Notes from a letter on Hospitals." The letter referred to is surely from Mrs. Congreve, whom George Eliot asked for information on " provincial hospitals, which is necessary to my imagining the conditions of my hero " on September 21, 1869,[22] ten days after she had completed chapter 3 of " Middlemarch." That same notebook entry also indicates that the semispaced pages of chapter 13 which concern the chaplaincy dispute not only were written later than chapter 3 of " Middlemarch " but were being written (or rewritten) during the first three months of 1871, while George Eliot was joining " Middlemarch " and " Miss Brooke." For the " Notes from a letter on Hospitals " are immediately followed in the notebook by two entries having to do with the fusion of the two stories: a list showing how the directors of the new hospital voted on the chaplaincy issue, one of the voters being a " Miss Brooke " character (Arthur Brooke, Dorothea's uncle), and a rough map of the Middlemarch area which includes Mr. Casaubon's parish, Lowick, and the estates of Mr. Brooke and Sir James Chettam, Tipton and Freshitt.

The first time the name of Mr. Farebrother, one of the candidates for the chaplaincy, appears, on page 137 (1: 190), George Eliot had to change it from an earlier version—" ' B⟨u⟩rrow's parish. You. . . .' " She made the change in the name, however, while writing the sentence, i. e., she deleted the erroneous passage and wrote the correct one on the same line without having to squeeze it in or insert it above the line. This indicates either a first draft or a copying from a previous draft. Other evidence makes the latter the more probable. The deleted numbers 145-50 on pages 140-45 are part of the joined *Middlemarch*, not part of the original " Middlemarch " pagination. This deleted series implies the existence of an earlier, regularly spaced beginning of this chapter (pages 135-44) . Semispaced pages 135-38 thus might be redrafts of approximately eight pages of an earlier draft written according to the ruled lines (numbered 135-42) ; page 139 might be a rewriting of an older page 143. The one-page discrepancy—the deleted number on page 140 is 145, not 144— can be accounted for as a result either of the small writing made necessary by semispacing or of condensation of the matter of the original.

What seems to have happened was something like this: while George Eliot was joining this portion of " Middlemarch " to " Miss Brooke," she realized that the Bulstrode-Lydgate conversation which in the old " Middlemarch " took place at some other point in the beginning of the novel might better be part of the same chapter which contained the Bulstrode-Vincy conversation. She inserted the original draft of these pages, regularly spaced, into this chapter of the manuscript and made those revisions necessary to join the two into a well-knit chapter. The pages of this new *Middlemarch* chapter she numbered 135-50. Then, either she conceived of still further connections between the two conversations, e. g., Vincy's inviting Lydgate to dinner, or the integration resulted in too messy a manuscript, so she rewrote or recopied the first part of the chapter, this time writing two lines of text per ruled line.

Whenever there is no evidence to the contrary it is convenient and reasonable to assume that the beginning of " Middlemarch " was very much like the present four, five, or six chapters following the last " Miss Brooke " chapter, chapter 10. But chapter 13 seems to fall into two parts, Bulstrode's conversation with Vincy and Bulstrode's conversation with Lydgate, and these two parts contain disparate mechanical characteristics— semispaced pages and renumbered pages. It seems more reasonable to assume that they came from different drafts and that this chapter as we now have it differs from its " Middlemarch " original. The integration effected was undoubtedly made necessary by the decision to join " Miss Brooke " and " Middlemarch." Indeed, if the first two chapters of " Middlemarch " dealing with the Fred-Featherstone story had prepared the way for the Lydgate-Bulstrode story as successfully as does chapter 13 of *Middlemarch*, there would seem to have been little reason for George Eliot to have delayed so long in her writing of " Middlemarch," as we know she did from September, 1869, to the first months of 1871.

The first two semispaced passages more or less satisfactorily accounted for, there remains only the third, the most difficult passage to identify. These pages (pp. 160-68) , comprise almost all of chapter 15. This chapter narrates Lydgate's pre-Middlemarch history: his childhood decision to become a physician, his medical education and ambitions for research and reform, and his infatuation and disillusionment with Laure, the French actress. Aside from the Parkins and Gotto pages which conclude this chapter (pp. 169-70) , there are indications that the chapter is a first draft: a number of the pages (pp. 161, 163, 164) are heavily revised, some have been rewritten,[23] and Lydgate's first name has been changed from

---

[23] Pages 165 and 165a, the latter containing only a half-page of writing; possibly page 160, which ends, " Still, I repeat, there was a general impression that Lydgate

"⟨Tristram⟩" to " Tertius " (see Illustration 2, Appendix A). But this evidence of a first draft is qualified, if not nullified, not only by the supposition that if the other semispaced passages are redrafts then this passage must be a redraft too, but by a concrete and conclusive sign: on the back of one of those pages which, because of the number of revisions, seem most clearly to be part of a first draft, page 163, there is a false start of more than two lines of writing, *spaced according to the ruled lines* and numbered " 170." Thus page 163 seems to have been written after a regularly spaced page 170 had been begun, though because of the illegibility of those deleted lines it is impossible to say where in the chapter this earlier page 170 occurred. Like the other semispaced passages, this chapter may be considered at least a second draft.

However, a second draft is not necessarily a recopying of the first; some parts of chapter 15 may be new in the second draft and thus belong to a period later than that of other parts of the chapter. The introductory nature of the chapter itself makes conjecture about its origin and the origin of its various parts difficult.

Obviously an introduction of Lydgate to the reader, this chapter may in fact be the " Introduction " to the original " Middlemarch " that we know was written but of which there is no trace unless in this chapter. Lydgate's choice of a career while still a child, some of his education, some of the description of the state of medical practice in the provinces at the time, even his experience with Laure might well have formed part of the " Introduction " to " Middlemarch." The last paragraph of the chapter as it now stands indeed sounds like the end of such an introduction:

No one in Middlemarch was likely to have such a notion of Lydgate's past as has here been faintly shadowed, and indeed the respectable townsfolk there were not more given than mortals generally to any eager attempt at exactness in the representation to themselves of what did not come under their own senses. Not only young virgins of that town, but grey-bearded men also, were often in haste to conjecture how a new acquaintance might be wrought into their purposes, contented with very vague knowledge as to the way in which life had been shaping him for that instrumentality. Middlemarch, in fact, counted on swallowing Lydgate and assimilating him very comfortably.

---

was something rather more uncommon " (1: 215), because the preceding sentence, " Nobody's imagination had gone so far as to conjecture that Mr. Lydgate could know as much as Dr. Sprague and Dr. Minchin, the two physicians, who alone could offer any hope when danger was extreme, and when the smallest hope was worth a guinea," was inserted in the bottom margin and placed by means of an arrow, a similar passage, now partially illegible, " No [one's] imagination had . . . to the supposition . . . that he might know more than even Dr. Sprague or Mr. Minchin, the two physicians [of] Middlemarch " having been inserted in the margin at the top of the next page and deleted; page 168 is almost completely free of revision and seems to have been rewritten.

What better lead could there be into the story of Lydgate's entrapment by both Bulstrode and Rosamond?

If, however, the *Quarry* material which George Eliot gathered in August and September of 1869 was necessary, e. g., for details such as the " recent legal decision " which permitted Lydgate to prescribe without taking a " cut " from the druggist (p. 165; 1: 223) and the work on tissues by Bichat (p. 165; 1: 224), she could not have written these pages when we know the " Introduction " to the original " Middlemarch " was written, in July, 1869. If these details were in the original version of this chapter, the chapter must have come after chapter 3, following Lydgate's meeting Rosamond as it now does. Similarly, the first page of this chapter (p. 160) is not introductory, since it assumes, especially in the second paragraph, Lydgate's having already met Rosamond:

At present I have to make the new settler Lydgate better known to any one interested in him than he could possibly be even to those who had seen the most of him since his arrival in Middlemarch. For surely all must admit that a man may be puffed and belauded, envied, ridiculed, counted upon as a tool and fallen in love with, or at least selected as a future husband, and yet remain virtually unknown.

It will also be noted that this paragraph is a remarkable foreshadowing *or echo* of the last paragraph of chapter 15 quoted above. Finally, the qualification of the phrase " fallen in love with "—" or at least selected as a future husband "—treats Rosamond with an irony and cynicism which may be a rather late insight of George Eliot's into her character. That George Eliot wrote these pages too late for them to have been part of the " Introduction " to " Middlemarch " does not mean that the rest of the chapter was not part of that introduction, for it is precisely these late pages which we have already identified, on the basis of their appearance in the manuscript (n. 22), as newer than the pages around them.

We may have pointed out three stages in the rewriting of this chapter. First, there was the original version of the chapter which George Eliot probably wrote in July, 1869, as the introduction to " Middlemarch," regularly spaced on the ruled lines of " 1869 " paper; she extensively revised and expanded this version during the early months of 1871 when she was joining " Middlemarch " to " Miss Brooke," adding some pages on Parkins and Gotto unlined paper, and numbering the pages 151-72. Second, there is the semispaced version, a revision of the first. Finally, there is the present version which resulted from George Eliot's rewriting the first page of the chapter (p. 160) once again and adding pages 165 and 165a.

Though there is no corroborating evidence in the British Museum manuscript, it is possible, because of the nature of the chapter, that

George Eliot considered other points in the novel for its appearance. For example, this chapter may have been the first complete " Middlemarch " chapter in the newly fused *Middlemarch*, following the dinner-party scene in chapter 10, and if it was indeed the introduction to the old " Middlemarch " this position would probably have been the first to occur to the author. Further, it might have appeared immediately after chapter 12, following the meeting of Lydgate with Rosamond and preceding both the conversations with Bulstrode (chap. 13) and Fred's giving the note to Featherstone (chap. 14). Finally, it could have appeared after chapter 16, following the dinner party at Vincy's in which both the Lydgate-Bulstrode and the Lydgate-Rosamond plots are furthered. The number of possible positions for this chapter makes it basic to the organization of this part of the novel but makes specific identification of its origin and reconstruction of its history extremely difficult.

Contributing to these difficulties are the two pages of Parkins and Gotto paper at the end of the chapter, the only two pages in chapter 15 with numbers which have been changed. There are various possible explanations for the use of Parkins and Gotto paper. These pages may have come from the original draft, and thus all " 1869 " pages are either copies or completely new. These pages may equally well belong to the immediate post-join, or bridge, period, i. e., to the same draft as the end of chapter 11 (breakfast scene) when George Eliot was recopying or writing new links between " Miss Brooke " and " Middlemarch " on this Parkins and Gotto paper; or the pages on Parkins and Gotto paper just " happened " to be used and indicate nothing.

There is little in the physical appearance of these pages which helps identify their origin. They are slightly freer from revision than is usual in the *Middlemarch* manuscript, though not so free as to show beyond doubt that they were copied from an earlier draft. There is a slight change in the writing and in the color of the ink near the middle of page 169 (1: 231, beginning with, " ' I know, I know,' said Lydgate, deprecatingly "), but occurring as it does in the middle of a scene and in the middle of a Parkins and Gotto page this does little to explain the presence of these two pages and would seem to indicate scarcely more perhaps than a pause in the writing or a shift of position by the writer, fatigue, or the beginning of a new day's writing. Page 169 is torn and pasted; but this could have occurred as easily at the printer's or between 1871 and the time I first saw the manuscript in 1951 as between 1869 and 1871. Finally, the page numbers " 169 " and " 170 " are written over what *probably* was " 171 " and " 172," though the last digits are almost illegible; this last is at first only baffling, but may, in the long run, help us to discover the origin of these pages.

To identify these Parkins and Gotto pages as part of the original draft of " Middlemarch " would seem to contradict the evidence of the " Dove " passages. To identify them simply as " sports " does not satisfy one's curiosity and is a last resort. To identify them as part of the bridge passage, written after George Eliot decided to join " Middlemarch " to " Miss Brooke," i. e., as having been written about the same time as were pages 97-112 (pages which are also on Parkins and Gotto paper) requires certain complex, even ingenious, but not incredible conjectures.

The point at which George Eliot exhausted her supply of Parkins and Gotto paper needs to be established. This point was not necessarily at page 113 where the " 1869 " paper makes its first appearance. Pages 113-19 and probably pages 113-24 are " Dove " passages predating the preceding bridge passages and have already been tentatively identified as a portion of the original " Middlemarch." Similarly, pages 140-45 (the Vincy-Bulstrode interview) and pages 146-54 (the second Fred-Featherstone scene) have been identified as portions of this older draft. Further, a large number of the intervening pages—pages 131-34, 135-38, and 160-68 (these are the earlier pages of chapter 15 preceding the Parkins and Gotto pages) —are semispaced. Since the Parkins and Gotto pages (pp. 169-70) have been renumbered and the semispaced pages of the chapter which precede them have not been renumbered, the Parkins and Gotto pages may be considered the earlier; if the semispaced pages and only these pages are part of the same draft, the Parkins and Gotto pages thus predate all other semispaced pages. Still further, pages 146-54 have been renumbered from 173-79 (and are, in addition, " Dove " pages) , which numbers follow those of the semispaced and Parkins and Gotto pages of chapter 15; chapter 14, then, may have been moved to its present place preceding chapter 15 only after chapter 15 had been rewritten and placed. Finally, the only intervening pages left unaccounted for are pages 125-30, the conversation between Mary and Rosamond, a passage which already has been identified as separate from the simultaneous Fred-Featherstone conversation on pages 120 ff. and apparently of much later origin than the " Middlemarch " pages which precede it; this passage may now be identified as having been written later than the end of chapter 15. Why this is so, and what conclusion this will lead to will be seen presently. Meanwhile, it is sufficient to note that with the use of " Middlemarch " passages on " 1869 " paper and with the possibility that much of the portion of the novel between the opening of chapter 11 and the end of chapter 15 was rewritten, it is possible that the supply of Parkins and Gotto paper was not exhausted until the end of chapter 15, and that these two pages belong to the bridge period when George Eliot was joining " Middlemarch " to " Miss Brooke."

It is perhaps convenient at this point to summarize the conclusions we have thus far been led to concerning the joining of the two earlier works into the beginning of *Middlemarch* and the evidence upon which these conclusions are based.

There seem to be five more or less distinct groups of pages in this portion. The first and easiest to identify contains the opening nine-plus chapters of the novel, which are almost certainly part and perhaps all of the original draft of " Miss Brooke." These pages are on Parkins and Gotto paper; where " Middlemarch " names appear, they have been substituted for deleted and now illegible originals.

The next group consists chiefly of the end of chapter 10, all of chapter 11, and the first page of chapter 12. These, also quite easy to identify, are bridge pages, evidently written to connect " Miss Brooke " to " Middlemarch." At the end of chapter 10, the dinner-party scene, characters from both stories appear, yet their names did not have to be inserted or revised in the manuscript. The beginning of chapter 11 explains how it is that Lydgate prefers Rosamond Vincy (from " Middlemarch ") to Dorothea Brooke; the latter half of the chapter, the Vincys at breakfast, may have been based upon an earlier draft but at least in its present form it seems to belong to this bridge period. Chapter 12 opens with one page that gets the young Vincys to Stone Court. All of these pages, like those of " Miss Brooke," are on Parkins and Gotto paper. " Miss Brooke " names appear in this " Middlemarch " section of the manuscript—even on the first page of chapter 12—without having had to be inserted. Much later, at the very end of chapter 15, there are two more Parkins and Gotto pages, the only other such pages in the entire *Middlemarch* manuscript; whether these too belong to the bridge draft is not clear, though there is no evidence that they do not.

Scattered through the remainder of this section of manuscript, from the second page of chapter 12 through the first half of chapter 16, are the other three groups of pages, all on " 1869 " paper and all concerning only " Middlemarch " characters. The extensive revising and rewriting evident throughout these chapters thus seem to have been necessary, not to join this story to " Miss Brooke," but to improve the presumably unsatisfactory beginning of " Middlemarch " itself.

In the first of these groups Mary Garth had been named " Dove." These pages seem to belong to the oldest " Middlemarch " draft in the British Museum manuscript: either they are copies of originals made before the bridge pages that now introduce them (in which Mary is surnamed " Garth "), or, as seems the more likely despite the absence of deleted " Middlemarch " page numbers, these are pages from the original draft itself. The " Dove " group is composed of at least two separated passages: the first extends for seven (or twelve) pages beginning with the second page of chapter 12 and comprises most or all of Fred Vincy's first conversation with Featherstone; the second makes up the beginning of chapter 14, the second Fred-Featherstone talk and the first part of Fred's conversation with Mary. Since all of the pages in this portion are on " 1869 " paper and many are regularly spaced, it is only where Mary's surname appears, as " Dove " or " Garth," that this " Middlemarch " draft can be identified. There are passages, however—the five pages following the first " Dove " passage in chapter 12 and the Vincy-Bulstrode interview in chapter 13 (part of the Fred-Featherstone plot development) —that seem to belong to the " Dove " draft.

The second of the three " Middlemarch " groups is easily recognizable: its pages are semispaced. Belonging to this group are the end of chapter 12 (the Rosamond-Lydgate meeting and the young Vincys on their way home from Stone Court), the Lydgate-Bulstrode interview in chapter 13, and all but the last two pages of chapter 15 (Lydgate's pre-Middlemarch history). Because of its subject matter (Fred-Featherstone, Rosamond-Lydgate) the first semispaced passage must have had a " Middlemarch " prototype, but because of its spacing and the appearance of an unrevised " Garth," the present passage seems to belong to a late, probably post-join draft. Since the sections of chapter 13 seem parts of different drafts and since the matter in the Lydgate-Bulstrode interview presupposes the regularly spaced Vincy-Bulstrode interview (but the latter does not pre-suppose the former), the semispaced passage in chapter 13 seems also to be of rather late origin; there was possibly a " Middlemarch " counter-part to the scene, a regularly spaced draft, though it probably came later in the story and was not part of that chapter which contained the Vincy-Bulstrode scene. The semispaced chapter 15 seems to be a much revised later draft of the original " Introduction " of " Middlemarch." Because of the repagination of the beginning of chapter 14 (which indicated that it once followed chapter 15) it appears likely that chapter 15 was once many pages longer, probably a regularly spaced draft. Several pages have evidently been added even after the chapter was semispaced, and the Parkins and Gotto final two pages of the chapter suggest that an even longer passage than these two pages had been added there; the additions contain details of the state of medical practice and research of the period and the Laure episode. All the semispaced sections (the end of chapter 12, the beginning of chapter 13, most of chapter 15) seem to be post-join drafts of " Middlemarch " passages adding new material. Though George Eliot seems to have rewritten these passages while joining " Middlemarch " to " Miss Brooke," she did so not to effect the fusion but to improve the unsatisfactory beginning of " Middlemarch."

The last of the three " Middlemarch " groups and the last of the five groups of manuscript pages in this section of the novel—what might loosely be called the " Garth " draft—is made up of miscellaneous passages in each of the chapters from 12 to 14. The first such passage is the Mary-Rosamond conversation in chapter 12, which seems to have been interpolated into the chapter to present Rosamond in a somewhat harsher light. The Vincy-Bulstrode passage in chapter 13 may belong to this draft but seems more likely part of the " Dove " group. The end of chapter 14, containing most of the Fred-Mary conversation, like the " Garth " passage in chapter 12, follows a " Dove " passage and like it seems to add new material to the Vincy plot line. In the " Garth " passages as in the semispaced ones, George Eliot evidently was trying to improve " Middlemarch " while incorporating it in the new novel; none of the rewriting directly concerns the joining of that story to " Miss Brooke."

This summary accounts for everything of note on these pages but the false start on a regularly spaced page 170 on the back of semispaced page 163, the continuing of the numbers of the pages of chapter 15 to 172, and the peculiar pagination of the beginning of chapter 16.

The lines on the back of page 163 do not seem to contain the same material as the beginning of page 163 itself nor of the semispaced page 170; though it cannot be identified definitely, the interrupted page 170 seems to belong somewhere toward the end of chapter 15. The writing of a semispaced page from near the beginning of the chapter on the other side of a discarded regularly spaced page from near the end of the chapter strengthens the conjecture that the semispaced pages are late in origin and presuppose, in one form or another, a former draft. The regular spacing on " 1869 " paper of the interrupted page from the latter half of the chapter suggests either that there was a regularly spaced earlier draft of this chapter, presumably from the original " Middlemarch," of which this is a discarded portion, or that George Eliot at one time intended writing or rewriting the latter portion of this chapter, possibly the Laure episode, in such a manner, and that therefore there may have been more Parkins and Gotto pages than just the two we now have.

Our choice between these two alternative hypotheses is not helped by the evidence of the repagination of the Parkins and Gotto pages, though that there are these two alternatives is confirmed. That chapter 15 extended to page 172 until very late in the writing of this section of the novel is indicated in *Quarry II*, 6, which, though it lists the chapters in their present order, indicates that chapter 15 ended even at this late date with page 172 and chapter 16 began with page 173. This list of chapters was made up after the decision to join " Middlemarch " and " Miss

Brooke," even after the decision to publish *Middlemarch* in parts, i.e., in the spring or summer of 1871. It is possible, therefore, either that some of the original pages of the "Middlemarch" manuscript occupied the present position of pages 167-68 and, because they were regularly spaced, took up four pages, 167-70, or, that these pages were then on Parkins and Gotto paper and were later adjusted to their present form—pages 167-68 semispaced and pages 169-70 simply renumbered to conform.

That the chapter following 15 began on page 173 is confirmed by the renumbering of the first pages of the present chapter 14 which once followed chapter 15, their original numbers, which began this inquiry in the first place, having been 173-79. Also, the first pages of the present chapter 16 are peculiarly numbered, indicating that even after chapter 14 was moved to its present position, chapter 15 ended with page 172: chapter 16 begins with a page numbered " 171, 172, 173, 174," none of these numbers being deleted. The succeeding pages are numbered " 175," " 175a," " 176," " 176a," " 177," and " 177a." What makes this numbering so peculiar is that there are exactly seven pages between 171 and 178, so that if these pages were numbered normally, page 178 would still be 178. What need was there to number the pages in this peculiar fashion?

Like so many other chapters in this portion of the novel, chapter 16 contains parts of more than one plot development: up to page 177a Lydgate hears the chaplaincy question discussed and himself tactlessly defends the necessity for a medical coroner, alienating the lawyers and physicians alike; the rest of the chapter is devoted to furthering his flirtation with Rosamond, though these pages are shot through with the presence of Mr. Farebrother and thus with a continuation of the chaplaincy dispute. Again the manuscript pages of these different plot sections contain different characteristics, which suggests that they originated in separate drafts or separate chapters.

The chaplaincy and coroner discussions are contained in and indeed end with the peculiarly numbered pages at the beginning of the chapter. Since the coroner discussion is in part based on George Eliot's reading in *Lancet* and recorded in *Quarry I* and the chaplaincy discussion on Mrs. Congreve's information requested on September 21, these discussions probably did not appear in that part of the novel written before September 11, 1869.

The origin of the Lydgate-Rosamond pages is less easy to fix. They have clearly been linked to the peculiarly numbered pages which precede them in this chapter and rather obviously predate those pages. Rosamond's presence is first indicated on the page that concludes the coroner and chaplaincy discussions, the last of the peculiarly numbered pages (p. 177a). This page and the first purely Rosamond-Lydgate page which follows it (p. 178) are remarkably free from revisions. Moreover, the heavily revised page 179, which continues the Rosamond-Lydgate flirtation, seems written in a slightly different handwriting, as if written at another time. It seems obvious, then, that pages 177a and 178 serve as links between the newer discussions scene and the older Rosamond-Lydgate scene. (The only mention of the previous meeting between Rosamond and Lydgate at Stone Court occurs on the "new" page 178. Is it possible that in the original "Middlemarch" the two were here meeting for the first time?)

Just as obviously, Mr. Farebrother's part in the middle of this chapter has been linked to the Rosamond-Lydgate pages. The core of the Rosamond-Lydgate scene after its introduction on the "clean" pages 177a-78 is contained in pages 179-81 and page 184.[24] All of these pages are much more heavily revised than are the pages which precede them, intervene, or succeed them. On the last, one revision may even indicate a pre-join origin for this scene: George Eliot has inserted the "Miss Brooke" phrase "towards Tipton and Lowick" (1: 246) and deleted a three-word phrase, the last word of which seems to be "country." Mr. Farebrother first appears on page 183, a "clean" page which has very obviously been joined to an already extant page 184. (The preceding page, p. 182, is also "clean," and may well have been rewritten in order to make the fusion of the Rosamond-Lydgate and Farebrother plot lines smoother.) He does not appear on the "older" page 184 but appears again on page 185, also a "clean" page, and his presence at the Vincys' is implied in Lydgate's first thoughts after leaving their house (at the top of p. 186 [1: 247], "'What is his religious doctrine to me . . .'").

Approximately the last third of this chapter (pp. 186-92) concerns Lydgate's notions of his relationship to Rosamond and her rather different notions of this same relationship. There is some evidence of rewriting even in this portion of chapter 16, but the rewriting seems to have little to do with the fusion of the various plot lines in the earlier portions of the chapter. Though there is no definite indication of which page was the earlier, there is evidence that page 187 has been joined to page 188, the last words of the former—"But these kinds of inspiration Lydgate regarded as rather vulgar and vinous" (1: 249)—having been repeated and deleted at the top of the latter. Moreover, this chapter extends through page 192, but the first pages of chapter 17 are marked "190a," "191b," and "192a," an obvious indication that chapter 16 once

---

[24] Pages 179-81 in the printed text run from 1: 241, "in thinking how lovely this creature was," to 1: 243, "one need not be surprised to find the rare conjunctions in nature"; page 184 begins on 1: 245, "Everything looked blooming and joyous," and ends on 1: 246, "said Rosamond, with a slight deprecatory laugh."

ended with page 189. This is confirmed by the list of chapter and manuscript page numbers on *Quarry II*, 6, which indicates that chapter 17
began on page 189. It is obvious, then, that George Eliot began chapter
17 before she completed the last part of chapter 16 as we now have it.
But the last part of chapter 16 is more or less of a coda in which she
summarizes and restates the Rosamond-Lydgate situation and solidifies
and deepens her presentation of it. There is, however, no action or scene
or new development, so that she could have added it at any time after
the beginning of chapter 17 without its revealing to us anything of the
relative age of chapters 16 and 17.

What we have in chapter 16, then, is: first, a core of pages dealing
with the Rosamond-Lydgate flirtation which may date back to the original " Middlemarch " and, indeed, in that work may have been the first
meeting between the two; second, a beginning, joined to the Rosamond-
Lydgate passage, having to do with the chaplaincy question and the
merits of a medically trained coroner; third, a few pages dealing with
the chaplaincy dispute through the introduction in person of one of the
parties to that dispute, Mr. Farebrother, which have been interspersed
through the Rosamond-Lydgate pages; and finally, a coda, much of which
had been added after chapter 17 had been begun, in which Lydgate, in
his rooms, thinks of Farebrother, of Rosamond, and most of all of his
experiments, and in which Rosamond's romance, which she has woven
around the person of Lydgate, is narrated.

Three of the four page numbers on the first page of this chapter can
be explained as having been made necessary by the shortening of chapter
15, which, though it once clearly extended to page 172, now ends with
page 170. Therefore, the first page of chapter 16 had to be numbered
" 171, 172, 173." The presence of " 174 " also on that page can only be
explained as a result of a paring down of an earlier version of the beginning of this chapter.[25] The numbering of the rest of these early pages

---

[25] The motto which in the printed text appears at the head of chapter 18
> " Oh, sir, the loftiest hopes on earth
> Draw lots with meaner hopes: heroic breasts,
> Breathing bad air, run risk of pestilence;
> Or, lacking lime-juice when they cross the Line,
> May languish with the scurvy."

in the manuscript once appeared on the first page of this chapter. How such a motto
is applicable to chapter 16 as it now stands is difficult to imagine. Perhaps the
chaplaincy and coroner discussions which now open chapter 16 once opened chapter
18, the chapter at the head of which this motto now stands and in which the chaplaincy
election takes place. The appearance of this inappropriate motto confirms the
conjecture that the chaplaincy and coroner disputes in this section of the manuscript
have been moved from some other portion of the novel to the opening of chapter 16
and joined with the Rosamond-Lydgate and other elements in this chapter.

of chapter 16—" 175," " 175a," " 176," " 176a," " 177," and " 177a "—suggests that at one time these pages were semispaced pages 175-77. This would be consistent with George Eliot's practice when fusing chapters or plot lines, if, as has been suggested above, these early pages were added to the core of pages dealing with Rosamond and Lydgate. It is even possible that these early pages went through three drafts—a regularly spaced first draft (perhaps as part of the original " Middlemarch "), a semispaced second draft as George Eliot tried to fuse them into this chapter, and a third and final draft, regularly spaced and relatively free of revisions but strangely numbered—the pages, in other words, that we now have.

The investigation of the altered numbers on the first pages of chapter 14 has led us to an investigation of all the semispaced pages and the entire network of evidence of origin in chapters 12-16. But we have still not answered the basic query of why certain pages were semispaced.

The most obvious answer would be that George Eliot squeezed these pages together in order to retain as much as possible of her pagination. This explanation would suit those first semispaced pages, 131-34, if pages 125-30 (the Mary-Rosamond conversation) were added to the original manuscript after chapter 13 had already been begun and numbered. In other words, the regularly spaced ending of chapter 12 occupied pages 125-34. When five more pages were inserted, it would have been necessary to remember the original pages 131-40. Since chapter 13, already begun, started with page 135, it was necessary to squeeze the ten regularly spaced pages into four semispaced ones. But *had those original pages been satisfactory in their original form*, it would have been easy simply to renumber them 131-34 and " 134a," " 134b," etc. Furthermore, chapter 13 already extended to page 150; when the early pages of chapter 13 were semispaced, they could have been renumbered 141-45, and the original page numbers of the end of that chapter, 145-50, could have been retained simply by designating the first as " 145a." So, even in the case of the first small section of semispaced pages, " squeezing " alone is not a satisfactory explanation of the semispacing.

It is even less satisfactory an explanation of the second section of semi-spaced pages, for here George Eliot had already numbered the succeeding pages as if these first pages were regularly spaced, so that the squeezing did not make the pagination conform but necessitated a change. Finally, if she semispaced chapter 15 so that she could insert chapter 14 before it, she could still simply renumber the pages of chapter 15 from 165 or so on, there no longer being a page 173 or succeeding pages to set the upper limits.

In other words, to explain the semispaced pages as having been made necessary in order to retain the original pagination is not only unconvincing on the surface—it is much easier to change page numbers than it is to rewrite, even to recopy, pages—but it is unconvincing in the specific cases of each of the three semispaced passages in this section of the novel.

If the original draft of what now are pages 131-34 had been satisfactory, there would have been no need to rewrite and semispace those pages. With the addition of pages 125-30 the original version of these pages was no longer satisfactory, for Rosamond's character and the conditions under which she met Lydgate had been changed, and it was necessary to combine this new version of her character and of the event with the older material. Therefore the function of the semispaced pages was *to combine.* In this first semispaced section, at least, there was an element of " squeezing," but without the need for combining new elements, this " squeezing " could have been accomplished simply by renumbering pages. The necessity for combination and its relationship to the semispaced pages is even more evident in the opening pages of chapter 13, where the Lydgate-Bulstrode conversation was combined with the Vincy-Bulstrode conversation; the new section is semispaced, the old regularly spaced. Similarly, in the semispaced chapter 15, what was apparently all or part of the old " Introduction " to " Middlemarch " was combined with new material about medical research and practices of the day and perhaps with the new Laure episode. Finally, the opening pages of chapter 16 dealing with the coroner dispute, which seem to have been semispaced at one time, were also being combined with the Lydgate-Rosamond courtship of the middle portion of that chapter. Thus the semispaced pages can all more or less be considered pages in which two or more elements of the plot of " Middlemarch " were being fused into a more integrated story line. This was not strictly part of the fusion of " Miss Brooke " and " Middlemarch," but was done as part of that fusion and obviously lifted George Eliot out of the doldrums into which she had fallen with the less well-integrated early chapters of the original " Middlemarch."

This explanation, though it defines the nature of the semispaced pages—it tells *what* they are—does not, except in the case of the first semispaced section, actually answer the question of why they were so written—*why* they are semispaced. Perhaps the necessity for " squeezing " while rewriting pages 131-34 set the pattern for the rewriting of those other passages in which two or more elements were being combined. Perhaps George Eliot felt that there was no need for space for revisions between lines of rewriting; perhaps she felt somehow that because these pages were being combined, the writing ought to be squeezed together; perhaps she felt the semispaced writing on a ruled page made such a page more nearly equal in length to the rather closely written pages on unlined paper; perhaps it was simply part of her mood during this part of the rewriting process. The question of her motives lies more in the realm of the psychologist than in that of the literary scholar.

None of the other passages in this part of the novel are semispaced because they do not share this combining characteristic: pages 113-24 are part of the original draft of " Middlemarch "; pages 125-30 are new to this pre-join draft but predate the semispacing though they cause the semispacing of the pages which follow; pages 140-45 are part of the original " Middlemarch " as is the first part of chapter 14, pages 146-54; pages 155-59 are new and not combining; pages 189-92 are new pages added to chapter 16, and pages 178-88 or 179-88 contain at least some pages from the original " Middlemarch " and so, though elements are being combined, there is no complete rewriting.

Though she revised extensively and rewrote some pages, nothing suggests that George Eliot wrote any of the chapters after chapter 16 either as part of " Miss Brooke " or as part of the original " Middlemarch." There are no more Parkins and Gotto pages, no more semispaced pages, no more revisions of proper names which suggest an attempt to combine or reconcile the characters or places of " Miss Brooke " and " Middlemarch," and no more appearances of the surname " Dove."

However, she rewrote a great deal of chapter 17, that chapter in which Lydgate visits Farebrother's house, meets his family, and discusses success and independence. Up to page 196 (1: 262: " turning on his heel and beginning to fill his pipe ") there are extraordinarily few revisions, a circumstance more strongly suggesting rewriting because of the appearance of two pages numbered " 195 " and " 195a." There is also a page 198a, but the page following it, which because of the numbering would appear to be one of the original pages of the chapter,[26] contains the names " Garth " and " Lowick " unrevised. If one of the oldest pages of this " Middlemarch " chapter contains a " Miss Brooke " name unrevised,

---

[26] Page 199 is rather free of revision but the pagination makes it appear to be one of the earlier pages of the chapter; page 196 is heavily revised and the name " Trawley," which appears here for the first time, has been changed from an illegible, deleted original, though " Trawley " appears on page 197 without need for revision; page 198 is rather heavily revised; page 200 has obviously been joined to a pre-existing, heavily revised page 201—not only is there a visible difference in the handwriting and the shade of ink used on the two pages, but the sentence, " They really look at the rest of mankind as a sort of carcass to nourish them for heaven " appears to have been deleted at the top of page 201 because it repeats the last phrase on page 200, " they really look on the rest of mankind as a doomed carcass which is to nourish them for heaven " (1: 267). If all four pages preceding page 201—198, 198a, 199, 200—

it obviously must have been written after the decision to join the two stories had been made. Indeed, there is no reason to believe this chapter was not written in its entirety after the decision to join the two stories. It comes late enough in the sequence of " Middlemarch " chapters to suggest that it was well beyond the third chapter of that work, which was as much as we know for certain was written; it deals with subject matter revealing a late enough stage in the planning of the novel to indicate that it was one of the chapters written as part of the joined *Middlemarch* but completed before March 19, 1871, when George Eliot had finished 236 pages of the novel.

Similarly, chapter 18, which shows signs of considerable rewriting within its pages, must nevertheless be considered part of *Middlemarch*. It deals with the election at which Lydgate impulsively sides with Bulstrode and votes for Tyke. One of the members voting is Dorothea's uncle, Arthur Brooke of Tipton, the first " Miss Brooke " character to appear on stage since chapter 10. All of the pages are on " 1869 " paper; none is semispaced. At the same time, because of the change of two character names (but not that of Mr. Brooke), this would seem to be a first draft. Finally, on *Quarry II*, 2, as we have seen, there is a list of the non-medical men voting, a list apparently made while or before this chapter was written, and Mr. Brooke's name appears in this list. This voting list is the first evidence in the notebook of the joining together of the two stories and would confirm the conjecture that chapter 18 is an early chapter of the newly joined *Middlemarch* written entirely as part of that work.

Chapter 23, once chapter 19, seems also to be a first draft and a post-join chapter. It is considerably revised throughout most of the first three-quarters of its length and shows no evidence of repagination or of extensive rewriting. There are two changes which should be noted, however. First, the public house called the Green Dragon appeared originally in this chapter as the White Horse. This same house appeared in chapter 18 as the Green Dragon without need for revision. This may be evidence of an oversight or of an attempt to " economize " by identifying the two houses as the same; it is not necessarily an indication that chapter 23 was written before chapter 18. Second, after page 234 (1: 363: " twenty sawyers. I never heard "), toward the end of the chapter, are four pages on which a total of no more than four revisions appear, far fewer than on each of the two pages immediately preceding this section of manuscript. The numbers of the first two of these pages, 235 and 235a, clearly

belong to a second draft, why is there not a 200a instead of a 198a? Thus page 199 would, with page 201, seem to be part of a first draft, despite the few revisions on page 199. The entire chapter thus seems to be of post-join origin.

indicate rewriting. *Quarry II*, 6, which lists the chapters of this part of the novel and the manuscript page numbers which each contains, indicates that this chapter at one time ended with page 236, not, as it presently does, with page 237. This proves not only that George Eliot rewrote the last four pages of this chapter, four pages replacing two, but that her March 19, 1871, journal entry stating that she had completed 236 pages of "my novel" refers to manuscript pages, despite the parenthetical interpolation of the word "print," and that it was this point, the end of the present chapter 23 (then chapter 19), that she had reached in writing *Middlemarch*.

This chapter, which returns our attention to the Fred-Featherstone plot, bears no signs of having been written during the "Middlemarch" period: it is written on "1869" paper following the twenty-three ruled lines; the name "Garth" appears without revision on at least six different pages in the early part of the chapter (pp. 220, 223, 224, 225, 226, and 229). Perhaps it was written before chapter 18, which contains the name of the Green Dragon unrevised, but probably not before the decision to join "Miss Brooke" to "Middlemarch."

On the last day of 1870, George Eliot, as was her custom, was reviewing her accomplishments of the past year. They were not very impressive. All she had at hand was about one hundred pages of a prose work which she had begun about two months before as a rather short story but which had by this time threatened to run to novel length. In order to devote her time to this new novel it appeared necessary to abandon a novel which she had begun in 1869 and of which she had written an introduction, three full chapters, and, perhaps, a chapter or two more. Reluctant to discard this older work completely, though she had interrupted it to write a poem and to begin a short prose work, she suddenly saw that it and the new novel she had begun were similar in setting and theme, similar enough, indeed, to make up parts of the same large novel.

Early in 1871 she set about joining these two works—the older and almost abandoned "Middlemarch" and the newer work, "Miss Brooke," which was outgrowing its initially conceived length. Of the latter, she had written ten chapters, carrying the main story from the meeting of Casaubon and Dorothea to their departure for Italy on their wedding journey and preparing the way for further developments through the introduction of Mr. Brooke's political ambitions and the presence of Casaubon's good-looking second cousin, Will Ladislaw. To accommodate "Miss Brooke" to the plan for the new *Middlemarch* was relatively easy: she could keep almost all of the manuscript without rewriting; she had only to write a new ending to chapter 10, introducing Mr. Vincy, Bulstrode, Lydgate, and other characters from "Middlemarch" at a dinner party just prior to Dorothea's departure for Italy, and had to change a few place-names to conform to the new locale, Middlemarch. Then Dorothea would be off stage and the "Middlemarch" portion of the novel could begin.

To join to this "Miss Brooke" beginning the fragments of the old "Middlemarch" was not so easy. For one thing, though "Miss Brooke" had progressed rather well, resulting in ten chapters in less than two months, "Middlemarch" had stalled more than a year earlier after just three chapters which, with the introduction, took a month and a half to complete. The "Introduction," written in July, 1869, apparently narrated Lydgate's boyhood discovery that the human anatomy operates on certain scientifically ascertainable mechanical principles, his decision to become a physician, perhaps some abstract summary of his education in Paris and his desire for research and reform, and perhaps also the episode with Laure. The first three chapters, written by September 11, presented, perhaps, a breakfast scene at the Vincys' similar to but not identical with the one in chapter 11 of *Middlemarch*; Mrs. Waule's gossipy and malicious remark to Featherstone that Bulstrode had claimed that their nephew Fred was paying gambling debts with promissory notes predicated on his inheriting Featherstone's property; the arrival at Stone Court of Rosamond and Fred Vincy; Featherstone's demand that Fred produce a note from Bulstrode that he did not believe Mrs. Waule's rumor to be true; the meeting, perhaps accidental, between Lydgate and Rosamond; Mr. Vincy's attempt to get the required note from Bulstrode for his son, and Fred's presentation of the note to Featherstone for which he received a badly needed but still inadequate gift of one hundred pounds.

In all probability little else, if anything, of what we have in *Middlemarch* was written prior to September 11, 1869. Perhaps, though, a little bit remains of what was written as part of "Middlemarch" after that date when the writing of that novel dragged on. At least from the fifth of August, George Eliot had been doing some research in medical subjects and the state of medicine in about 1830, when the action of the novel was to have taken place. The dispute over the relative merits of a medically trained and a legally trained coroner which at present appears near the beginning of chapter 16 was based on one of the earliest medical notes in *Quarry I* taken from *Lancet* and could have been written, though not in its present form, prior to September 11. Similarly, the few pages left of the early draft of the scene at Vincy's in which the Rosamond-Lydgate flirtation is furthered, also in chapter 16 now, could have been written prior to that date. But we cannot be certain; we know little about the nature of the early "Middlemarch." About this date, apparently,

George Eliot conceived the idea of connecting Bulstrode and Lydgate through the chaplaincy of the new hospital. On September 21, more than a week after she had completed the third chapter, she asked Mrs. Richard Congreve—whose father, Dr. Bury, was the attending physician to Robert Evans, George Eliot's father, during his last illness—for information concerning provincial hospitals. Thus if she wrote the conversation between Bulstrode and Lydgate about the chaplaincy (now in chapter 13) as part of the original " Middlemarch " at all, it must have been after Mrs. Congreve answered her questions. So, too, the coroner dispute as it now stands, intertwined as it is with that chaplaincy dispute, George Eliot could not have written during the time when we know she wrote the first three chapters of " Middlemarch."

Much of the matter which now forms chapters 11-17 of *Middlemarch* was already at hand and already embodied in the first draft of " Middlemarch." What caused the difficulty early in 1871 in writing this part of the novel *Middlemarch* was not so much joining " Middlemarch " to " Miss Brooke," for there are no " Miss Brooke " characters involved in the action of this part of the novel until Mr. Brooke appears at the Tyke-Farebrother election in chapter 18, but in recreating the apparently unsuccessful and unstimulating beginning of " Middlemarch." Apart from the dinner-party scene in chapter 10 and the opening pages of transition in chapter 11, little was needed to carry the action from " Miss Brooke " to " Middlemarch." But what amounted to a fresh beginning had to be made on " Middlemarch."

First, it seems that George Eliot changed her presentation of Rosamond's character and actions. Almost every scene in which Rosamond appears in this part of the novel can be identified as a later-than- " Middlemarch " draft. The breakfast scene in chapter 11, with which the " Middlemarch " portion of the novel begins, definitely belongs to the bridge period, though it may have been based on a " Middlemarch " version; in this scene Rosamond's imperiousness and her deliberate planning to meet Lydgate are revealed. Her conversation with Mary Garth on pages 125-30 had also been added some time after the rest of the chapter was written; this passage again presents Rosamond as complacent and vain, putting her in a particularly poor light by contrasting her with the intelligent and forthright Mary, and shows once again how she schemes to meet Lydgate, here questioning Mary about the young doctor. Finally, the very scene of the first Lydgate-Rosamond meeting, pages 131 ff., is semispaced and obviously a relatively late draft; here again, Rosamond is treated ironically, almost disdainfully:

> Mr. Lydgate was rather late this morning, but the visitors stayed long enough to see him; for Mr. Featherstone asked Rosamond to sing to him, and she herself was so kind as to propose a second favourite song of his (1: 174)

or again,

Nothing escaped Lydgate in Rosamond's graceful behavior: how delicately she waived the notice which the old man's want of taste had thrust upon her by a quiet gravity, not showing her dimples on the wrong occasion, but showing them afterwards in speaking to Mary, to whom she addressed herself with so much good-natured interest, that Lydgate, after quickly examining Mary more fully that he had done before, saw an adorable kindness in Rosamond's eyes. But Mary from some cause looked rather out of temper (1: 174-75).

Among those scenes in which Rosamond appears which could possibly be considered part of the original "Middlemarch" draft, only the scene at the Vincy home (in chapter 16) presents her with anything like the irony of these passages, and, unless this scene was, in the original "Middlemarch," the occasion of the first meeting of Lydgate and Rosamond, it apparently came fairly late in that draft. George Eliot herself later told her husband that Rosamond was one of the most difficult characters for her to sustain.[27]

The enriching of the early chapters of "Middlemarch" with new background material in the way of details of medical history and practice, the apparently new view or new presentation of Rosamond's character and the nature of her meeting with Lydgate, and the integration of the various plot strands were all parts of the task of George Eliot's blending of "Middlemarch" with "Miss Brooke" in chapters 11-16. The story of this part of the blending thus seems to go something like this:

The breakfast scene which completes chapter 11, which may or may not have been part of the first chapter of "Middlemarch," George Eliot wrote or rewrote presenting, among other things, a new view of Rosamond's character and revealing the deliberate nature of her scheme to meet Lydgate. Then, after the first page of chapter 12, which establishes the new geography of *Middlemarch* complete with Casaubon's parish of Lowick, the author salvaged five to ten pages of the original draft of "Middlemarch," or the earliest recopying of that original draft, presenting Mrs. Waule and her rumor, the arrival of Fred and Rosamond, and Featherstone's request. George Eliot then added five new pages of a conversation between Rosamond and Mary Garth (correctly surnamed) near the end of the chapter, again revealing Rosamond's character and her motives in coming to Stone Court. The author based the final pages of the chapter on the original "Middlemarch" but revised them extensively—in part to combine the new view of Rosamond with the older elements of the Fred-Featherstone plot—and in this draft semispaced them. Then, as a measure of artistic economy and integration, she fused the "Middlemarch" Bulstrode-Lydgate conversation which, if it appeared

[27] *Life* 3: 425.

in the original at all appeared later than this point, with the Vincy-Bulstrode conversation which was apparently part of the first two chapters of the old " Middlemarch." In this chapter, 13, the former conversation also gives Vincy an opportunity to invite Lydgate to dinner, having been prompted to do so by Rosamond in a " new " section of the text, and thus it prepares for the dinner scene in chapter 16. The Lydgate-Bulstrode conversation, like the end of chapter 12, is semispaced, but the older Vincy-Bulstrode conversation is regularly spaced. Chapter 14, which was to have followed 15 but was moved up, contains Fred's presenting the note to Featherstone, receiving a hundred pounds (scenes from the early parts of the old " Middlemarch "), and, apparently in a new section of manuscript, his conversation with Mary Garth which reveals their love and the chief obstacle to that love. Chapter 15 apparently includes the old " Introduction " to which the author added more specific details concerning medicine, research, and reform which she gleaned from her reading, with some additional linking material made necessary by the new position of the chapter in the novel; all but the last two pages of this chapter are semispaced and belong to the same " combining " draft as the last pages of chapter 12 and the opening pages of chapter 13, both of which sections are also semispaced. Chapter 16, like chapter 12, seems to be a composite of at least two earlier chapters or fragments of chapters, though it is not certain how much, if any, belongs to the " Middlemarch " period. In this chapter the scene in which the qualifications of a coroner are discussed, if it was written early in the " Middlemarch " period, has been combined with a discussion of the chaplaincy question and both have been fused to the Lydgate-Rosamond flirtation scene, the entire chapter then being extended.

This would appear to be the end of the debt *Middlemarch* owes to the original draft of " Middlemarch." The semispaced pages, the references to Mary " Dove," the revised " Miss Brooke " names in the " Middle-march " sections and vice versa—the criteria upon which this reconstruction has largely been based—disappear from the manuscript. Chapter 17, Lydgate's visit to Farebrother, has been extensively revised and rewritten, but there is no indication that any part of it belongs to the pre-join period. Chapter 18, containing the Tyke-Farebrother election, includes Dorothea's uncle in a speaking role. For the first time since the dinner party in chapter 10, characters from both portions of the novel mingle. They are to do so more frequently from this point on. By March 19, 1871, George Eliot reached the end of the next chapter, then 19, now 23. Though perhaps some of the final revisions described above were yet to be done, *Middlemarch* was now one novel.

CHAPTER TWO

Chapters 19–32: Publication in Parts

Though by March 19, 1871, George Eliot had decided to put together the beginnings of " Middlemarch " and " Miss Brooke " and though she had by that date reached page 236 in the resultant novel, much revision of the earlier portion and considerable planning of what was yet to be written still had to be done, for, as far as we know, she completed only nineteen more pages in the next three months.[1] Yet it was not primarily the fusing of the two stories into one which bothered her. There is no sign, at least, in the *Middlemarch* notebook of a struggle to unite the stories except through such superficial details as geography or through minor characters. Even on *Quarry II, 3*, where George Eliot lists " Relations to be developed," only the last two of the eleven desired relationships bring together characters from the two parts of the novel and these are vague and relatively unimportant: " of Caleb Garth to Mr. Brooke etc." and " of Mr. Farebrother to all, except Sir J. and Mr. Brooke."

It was length she was concerned with. Already on March 19 she feared she had " too many *momenti* "; by May she was sure of it. The new *Middlemarch* would need more room than even the three-decker format could afford.

This was not going to be good news to John Blackwood. The market for novels seemed sluggish. The English rights for five years to George Eliot's previous novel, *Felix Holt*, had cost him five thousand pounds,[2] yet in the conventional three-decker first edition he had sold scarcely 5,000 copies, did worse in cheaper later editions, and altogether must have lost a considerable sum on the venture.[3] How would he feel about publishing a new novel in four volumes? They might try small monthly parts, the form of issue Dickens and Thackeray had used successfully for such longer-than-usual novels as *David Copperfield* and *Vanity Fair*,

[1] George Eliot read Book 2 to George Henry Lewes on June 27, 1871, according to his diary (Anna Theresa Kitchel, *George Lewes and George Eliot* [New York, 1933], p. 259). Book 2 at this time ended with the chapter then considered 21 (now 25). I will soon deal at length with the shift involving these and other chapters in this portion of the novel; the last page of that chapter in the manuscript is numbered 255.

[2] *Letters* 4: 243. The terms of the agreement were not clear, but George Eliot later generously offered to include American and translation rights (*Letters* 4: 252).

[3] *Letters* 4: 318. See Haight, n. 2, p. 309.

but George Eliot always objected to having her work cut up into little bits [4] and the small sixpenny parts reissue of George Eliot's earlier novels, a recent experiment, had failed.[5]

Lewes came up with an idea. He sprang the need for four volumes and the idea in the same letter to Blackwood, May 7, 1871:

Mrs. Lewes finds that she will require 4 volumes for her story, not 3. I winced at the idea at first, but the story must not be spoiled for want of space, and as you have more than once spoken of the desirability of inventing some mode of circumventing the Libraries and making the public *buy* instead of borrowing I have devised the following scheme, suggested by the plan Victor Hugo followed with his long *Misérables* [6]—namely to publish it in *half-volume parts* either at intervals of one, or as I think better, two months. The eight parts at 5/- could yield the 2£ for the four volumes, and at two month intervals would not be dearer than Maga. Each part would have a certain unity and completeness in itself with separate title. Thus the work is called *Middlemarch*. Part I will be *Miss Brooke*.

John Blackwood and his nephew William visited the Leweses on May 31 and the publisher read Book 1 (then made up of the first ten chapters only) a few days later while still in London. It is reasonable to assume that also on this visit Blackwood agreed in principle to the Lewes plan of bimonthly publication, which was later carried out in every detail: number of parts, price, interval between parts. No such agreement appears in the correspondence, but when Blackwood wrote on July 20, after he had read Book 2 in manuscript, he seemed to assume the plan of publication: " I think our plan of publication is the right one as the two parts are almost distinct, each complete in itself. Indeed there will be complaints of the want of the continuous interest of a story, but this does not matter where all is so fresh and true to life." Early in September Blackwood agreed with Lewes's proposed terms of publication: the author was to get a forty per cent royalty on each part sold of the new novel. But meanwhile the " lack of a continuous story " and other considerations of parts publication had begun to exert their influence on the form *Middlemarch* itself was taking. By the time George Eliot had finished Book 3 in late October the demands of the new form of publication were becoming familiar to her; she wrote the later parts for half-

---

[4] *Letters* 6: 179.

[5] *Letters* 4: 372.

[6] According to Maurice Allem's " Notice Bibliographique," in *Les Misérables* (Paris, 1951), pp. 19-20, *Les Misérables* was published in volumes in Brussels as follows: Vols. 1 and 2 on March 30, 1862; 3-6 on May 16 (the " Notice " reads " mars," obviously a misprint for " mai "); 7-10 on June 30. In Paris the three dates of publication were April 3, May 15, and June 30. Thus Lewes got from the publication of *Les Misérables* only the general idea of publishing a long novel in large parts, not the details of quantity or interval.

volume issue without having to revise them into suitability. Therefore it is within Books 2 and 3 where we may find evidence of the influence of the form of publication, if there was any, on *Middlemarch*.

It is generally assumed that parts publication of a novel is detrimental to its structure and unity, forcing upon the author considerations other than the inherent nature of his material and his talent. This is not the case, however, with *Middlemarch*. It was to some extent to accommodate the prospective length of the new novel that Lewes proposed his plan for bimonthly parts. Moreover, about the time he made his suggestion, *Middlemarch* was made up of two contiguous but almost unrelated parts. The first, ten chapters long, until the middle of the last of those chapters dealt exclusively with " Miss Brooke "; it was, in fact, the opening of the original, independent " Miss Brooke," scarcely revised. The second, from nine to eleven chapters long at this time, was, except for the appearance of Mr. Brooke in chapter 18, an almost equally independent " Middlemarch " section. It surely was these half-volume sections which suggested the idea of half-volume parts to Lewes. Thus the publication form was originated to fit the fiction, not, at least at this stage, the fiction written to fit the form.

The new form did not have the rigid requirements of uniform and limited length which small parts issue did. *Middlemarch* parts were fewer in number, larger, and more expensive than those of previous novels issued in parts. *David Copperfield*, for example, appeared in twenty parts, each thirty-two pages long and selling for a shilling; the eight parts of *Middlemarch* varied from 174 to 212 pages in length and sold for five shillings each.[7] George Eliot was never forced to make a decision like this:

---

[7] When Book 1 of *Middlemarch* appeared on December 1, 1871, this form was new, though Graham Pollard in *Serial Fiction*, part of *Aspects of Book Collecting* (London, 1938), mentions Lytton's *The Parisians* (1871) as well as *Daniel Deronda* (1876) and Trollope's *The Prime Minister* (1876) as having appeared in this form. If the form was Lewes's idea as expressed in his May 7, 1871, letter to Blackwood, it seems unlikely that another novel by another author could have appeared in this form in that same year, apparently anticipating George Eliot. *The Parisians* ran as a serial in *Blackwood's Magazine* in sixteen installments from October, 1872, to January, 1874, and it is the serial which is given credit for first publication in the first book edition which Blackwood published in 1873. I have been unable to find notice of the Lytton novel appearing in half-volumes or in paper covers in this or any other year, though Blackwood wrote his nephew on November 2, 1871: " Lord Lytton I can put straight, as the plan of G. Eliot's novel was entirely their proposition. I remember something of a discussion about form for some of his Novels and I was in favour of trying the French system but Simpson was afraid of the paper covers," and Haight notes (5: 190-91) that Simpson wrote Blackwood on September 19, 1871, " enclosing specimen pages and a dummy of 208 pp. of ' the present shape of the Parisian Novel,' which looked better than the 176 pp. of the earlier calculations."

When the proofs of Part III reached him, Dickens found that he had overstepped his monthly allowance of thirty-two pages by thirty-five lines of type. Something had to be sacrificed, and this [description of David's mother's funeral] was one of the passages cut. It involves a small but appreciable relaxing of the tension.[8]

There is no evidence that Blackwood ever expressed displeasure at the length of the novel or that he ever made "tentative suggestions for cutting." [9] Cross's version of part of a letter from George Eliot to the publisher, July 24, 1871, does give the impression that Blackwood had suggested some changes:

> Thanks for the prompt return of the M. S., which arrived this morning.
> I don't see how I can leave anything out, because I hope there is nothing that will be seen to be irrelevant to my design.[10]

But Cross had removed from between the two sentences the following passage:

> I have just been making a calculation of the pages and I find, on a liberal estimate, that this second portion is about 190 pp. of the size you usually give to my novels—I think, 25 lines per page, is it not? "Miss Brooke" being about 150 pp. the two parts together would be equal to the larger volumes of Adam Bede and The Mill, which are at least 350 pp. if my memory may be trusted.
> Mr. Lewes has been saying that it may perhaps be well to take in a portion of Part II at the end of Part I. But it is too early for such definite arrangements.

Blackwood's letter of July 20, 1871, to which this was an answer, contained three pages of detailed praise of the second part and continued:

> I return the precious M.S. registered. Have you observed how much closer and smaller you are writing? When you can spare the M.S. I should like to have the quantity calculated. I am pretty sure there is equivalent to a volume of an ordinary novel in what I now return.

It was to this last sentence the author answered that, "the two parts together would be equal to the larger volumes of Adam Bede and The Mill." There was no suggestion for cutting; Blackwood's primary concern was to have some idea of the printed length of the parts before setting up type. Advance calculation was made difficult by the irregularity of George Eliot's writing and spacing, about which Blackwood complained. She answered some two months later, on October 29, 1871, "I hope in future to keep my pages tolerably equal, so as not to be in doubt about the size of my two-monthly Parts."

One of the reasons George Eliot did not want to be in doubt about

---

[8] John Butt, "The Composition of *David Copperfield* (I)," *The Dickensian*, 46 (Spring, 1950), 94.

[9] Blanche Colton Williams, *George Eliot* (New York, 1936), p. 259. Bullett, p. 220, refers to the same letter in the *Life* on which this interpretation is based and suggests that it is an answer to "her publisher's misgivings about the length."

[10] *Life* 3: 137.

the size of the parts was spelled out by Lewes in his letter to Blackwood on September 11: " Before setting up in type it will be well to have pages of the closely printed, less closely printed, and still less closely printed m.s. set up in order to form a calculation of quantity. The book must not *look thin* for 5/- and one must therefore see how many handsome pages it will make." This concern for " thickness" had already caused Lewes to suggest on September 7, 1871, a plan that would both pad and pay:

By the way a thought strikes me. Would it not be well to have an advertisement sheet bound up with each part—as Dickens & Thackeray had with their parts? (though not of course on the *covers*). This would not only bring in some hard cash, it would help make the volume look bigger for the 5/- which in British eyes is a consideration not to be neglected.

Blackwood, too, was concerned primarily with the outward bulk of the parts rather than with having a uniform number of pages in each. While George Eliot was concerned about the proportionate length of parts— " we think of sending the M.S. of Parts II & III to Edinburgh this week, that they may be got into type, to test their proportionate quantities " (October 29, 1871) ; " the Third Part is two sheets less than the First . . . it irks me to ask 5– for a smaller amount than that already given at the same price " [11]—the publisher insisted that the value of the part made up for what it lacked in length, and, on February 25, 1872, he was quick to offer a plan to insure the appearance of equality of length among the parts: " Do not disturb yourself about Book III being thin—there is the matter of volumes in it. . . . Besides the acute Simpson is using paper for the part which will make it bulk about the same as the others." This correspondence presents the rather peculiar but pleasant picture of the author concerned over the practical matter of the length of the parts and the publisher discounting this consideration and implying that only the effectiveness of the writing, " the matter of art," was important.

With but one exception, there was no mention of length of parts in the correspondence after the discussion of Book 3, but the author's notebook gives evidence of her continued concern. On *Quarry II*, 5-15, George Eliot listed chapters, grouped them into parts, and recorded after each part its total number of manuscript pages: 1: 134; 2: 126; 3: 150; 4: 164; 5: 151; 6: 156; 7: 149. When she began to write twenty-three lines to the manuscript page consistently, i. e., after Book 2, the variation between the parts in number of manuscript pages became slight, except for Book 4, a matter of but seven pages. Even this variation would have been less

---

[11] *Letters* 5: 249. Book 3 is 173 pages long; Book 1, 212 pages plus a three-page " Prelude." The difference of 39 pages without the " Prelude " is thus somewhat more than two sheets, i. e., 32 pages.

had she not added six pages to Book 6.[12] It is obvious that at least after Book 4 George Eliot was aiming at parts of 150 manuscript pages. (Even Book 8, though its total number of manuscript pages was not recorded in the notebook, contains 150 pages of manuscript excluding the " Finale.") This uniformity of the length of parts seems to have grown directly out of the actual publishing conditions, for (1) it becomes apparent with Book 5, (2) Book 5 is the point at which page numbers are begun anew with the first page of each part, and (3) Book 5 was the first begun after the publication of the first part.[13]

Manuscript page numbers also appear after many of the chapter titles listed in this part of the notebook—after every chapter in Books 1 and 2, after chapters 38-40 in Book 4, after chapters 63-68 in Book 7, and after chapters 80-85 in Book 8. Many of these numbers also indicate George Eliot's concern for the lengths of volumes or parts. She recorded the number of manuscript pages in each chapter of the first two parts evidently to help her estimate for the publisher the printed length of the first volume (that same estimate Cross omitted from the July 24, 1871, letter). Here she had to calculate chapter by chapter instead of by the total number of pages in the volume because of the irregular spacing of the lines in this portion of the manuscript. When she began to write more regularly, therefore, the number of pages in each chapter was unimportant and did not have to be recorded in the notebook. The total number of manuscript pages in the volume, on the other hand, became more important, so that she began to number her pages from the beginning of the volume instead of from the beginning of the novel. This she decided to do, apparently, while in the midst of writing chapter 37. Here she abandoned the original series—which had reached page 466 (ending, 2: 140, " nothing to be said against her husband except that he ") —renumbered the pages from the beginning of the volume—so that page 466 became 217 in the new series [14]—and continued from page 218

<hr/>

[12] 3: 134: " what sacrifice he could stay the rod," to 3: 140, " My mother felt it, and tried." George Eliot numbered the pages 130a-f of Book 6.

[13] *Life* 3: 144: " Dec. 1, [1871]—This day the first part of ' Middlemarch ' was published. I ought by this time to have finished the fourth part, but an illness . . . has robbed me of two months."

[14] In *Quarry II*, this chapter is 36. All chapter numbers in this part of the notebook are one lower than those in the published text.

The first page in the new series is 59, opening chapter 26. This manuscript page is only half-full, obviously a new page linking the new sequence of chapters after 19-22 and 23-25 were, as we shall see, switched. The next page is 60 in the new series and 347 in the old series. There are no new series pages 1-58, but chapters 19-22, which were originally intended as the opening of Book 3, contain just that number of pages. Chapters 23-25, which now open the part, contain but 38 manuscript pages. George Eliot must have begun the new series before transposing the chapters. She used the new series straight through the volume, i. e., through both Books 3 and 4.

to the end of the volume with the new series of page numbers. She then recorded in her notebook the new series number of the last page of the next chapter (chap. 38) and of those chapters that were then the last three in the volume (chaps. 39-41), apparently in order to get used to the new sequence, though conceivably to test out the length of Book 4, and therefore of the volume, should it end with any of these chapters.

Page numbers for chapter 42 do not appear in the *Quarry*; George Eliot numbered the pages in this last chapter of Book 4 " x " (i. e., " 1 ") through 18, obviously intending it as the opening of Book 5. After finishing chapter 45, which ended on page 60, she decided to move chapter 42 back to Book 4—possibly to lengthen the second volume—and therefore repaged what she had written of Book 5 without this chapter; chapter 45 now ended with page 40. With Book 6 the page numbers in manuscript begin again at one, for she was evidently now concerned about length of parts rather than about length of volumes. The apparently haphazard notation of page numbers for some chapters in the *Quarry* can thus be attributed to George Eliot's decision to discontinue numbering pages consecutively from the first page of the novel through to the end and instead to number the pages according to the volume. This procedure in turn gave way in Book 5 or 6 to beginning the page numbers anew with each part. Even the numbering of the pages thus indicates George Eliot's growing awareness of the importance of the half-volume parts format in the construction of the novel. It was not necessarily part length, however, which caused her to record page numbers after the first six chapters of Book 7 and after six of the last seven chapters of Book 8; perhaps these numbers are evidence of the author's concern for her progress toward completion of the novel.

If George Eliot did indeed aim at 150-page parts, there is no evidence of the precise nature of the effect of this aim on the novel. There is evidence that the aim was a very rough one and that there was no pressure from the publisher for absolute uniformity. There is a conspicuous absence of evidence of any direct effect of this aim on any individual passages in the novel. There is, indeed, evidence to the contrary: six pages were added to Book 6 despite the unequalizing of quantity the addition necessitated; manuscript page totals recorded by the author, except in the case of these six pages, do not even take into account addi-

---

The length of Book 4—164 pages in manuscript—which George Eliot achieved by including in it what had been intended as the opening chapter of Book 5, Chapter 42, might have been an attempt to compensate within the volume for the brevity of Book 3. Even so, this second volume in the first edition is considerably shorter than the first (372 pages compared to 402), though nearly equal to and indeed longer than the third and fourth volumes—363 and 367 pages.

tions, e. g., pages 17a, 40a, and 96a in Book 6, or erroneous numberings, e. g., two pages numbered " 3 " and two " 76," one page numbered " 141 & 142," and no pages 49 or 61 in Book 5. Even if we discount the variations in the printed lengths of the first four parts—212 pages, 196 pages, 173 pages, 199 pages—the variation in length of at least one of the last four parts is considerable—189 pages, 190 pages, 174 pages, 193 pages— and suggests that neither publisher nor author was too rigid in his attempts to keep the lengths of the parts uniform. Therefore, while the length of the parts must have been in the author's mind and may have exerted some influence on the development of the novel in her mind, the requirement of uniform length in the half-volumes was not exacting enough to change her actual writing of scenes or sentences.

If the novel could have been interrupted in mid-scene, mid-paragraph, or mid-sentence, there would have been no difficulty in maintaining parts of exactly equal length. But the half-volumes were units in themselves, and how to end them was a necessary consideration in view of their proposed bimonthly publication. In his letter of September 7, 1871, Lewes informed Blackwood that:

We have added on to the end of part I that portion of part II which closes with the scene at the miserly uncle's [chaps. 11 and 12]—a capital bit to end with; and this new arrangement not only pitches the interest forward into part II & prepares the way for the people & for Dodo's absence from part II, but also equalizes quantities better, though making part I rather longer than II which however is desirable.

In this one letter Lewes summarizes most of the necessary considerations and their interrelationships in the half-volume parts form of publication: the more nearly equal the length of the parts the better; equality of part length, however, is not important enough a reason to rewrite a portion of the novel or lessen the effectiveness of the ending of a part; the ending of a part should give the effect of the completion of one aspect of the novel (" a capital bit to end with "), should " pitch the interest forward," and should foreshadow the nature of the forthcoming part (" prepares the way "). The change necessitated by the considerations in the case Lewes was discussing, as in all such cases in *Middlemarch*, did not materially alter the novel. The chapters involved, 11 and 12, remained in the same order and form as they would have had the novel not been published in parts; they are now merely the concluding chapters of Book 1 rather than the opening chapters of Book 2.

George Eliot considered changes in the present endings of both Books 3 and 7 but decided against them on the basis of the " effectiveness " of the present endings, despite the fact that in both cases the change would have made the quantities less unequal. When she expressed concern over the fact that Book 3 was two sheets less than Book 1, Lewes "insisted that the death of Featherstone was the right point to pause at . . . in spite of diminished quantity," [15] and in spite of the fact that Book 2 was 196 pages long and 3 but 173. When "Lewes said something about changing the division" of Books 7 and 8, Blackwood suggested that "there might be a break at page 194, which would make Book 8 begin with 'In Middlemarch a wife could not long remain ignorant that the town held a bad opinion of her husband,'" but reconsidered in a post-script to the same letter: "On thinking over the division of the Books I feel that Dorothea's declaration of standing by Lydgate is so good an opening for what is to be expected in the last book that it is the most appropriate finish for Book 7, so that I would not mind making the one Book thin and the other thick." [16] Once again the desirability of the ending of one part preparing the way for the next won out over mere consideration of the relative lengths of the parts. As in the division of Book 1, neither of these contemplated changes would have affected the order of the chapters or the nature of any of the scenes of the novel.

George Eliot did have to take the endings of the parts into account in planning the novel, but this did not prevent the development of the novel from changing while she wrote. On *Quarry II*, 31, written while she was trying to sketch out the last three parts of *Middlemarch*, she was planning "*How to End the Parts*"—"Part VI ends with the Farebrothers telling Dorothea of Will's sudden departure. VII Ends with Lydgate's bribe [*written in above*: outpouring] to Dorothea. VIII Epilogue of reconciliation with Dorothea's family"—but these "statements . . . differ greatly from the endings of Book VI and VII as they were published. Will's departure (end of Book VI) is dramatically presented, not narrated by the Farebrothers. Book VII ends with the scene of Bulstrode's disgrace, followed by a short scene in which Dorothea declares her faith in Lydgate." [17] Thus George Eliot was not bound by her notion of how the parts had to be ended but changed these endings to suit the needs of the novel as these needs became apparent. The manner in which the parts were to be ended, like the relative equality of the lengths of the

---

[15] *Letters* 5: 249.

[16] *Letters* 5: 307-8. Book 7 contained 174 printed pages, Book 8, 193, including the 14-page "Finale" plus a 62-page catalogue of Blackwood publications. Had this change been made, Book 8 would have begun with chapter 74; Books 5, 6, and 7 would then have been 189 pages, 190 pages, and 190 pages, with Book 8, only 176 pages long, thickened by the catalogue.

George Eliot suggested on August 4, 1872, that "it will perhaps be desirable to make a few excisions [in Book 7] in order to introduce a little further development and leave larger room in the last Part," but I find no evidence of such excisions.

[17] Kitchel, p. 17.

parts, while clearly present in George Eliot's mind, had an indeterminable effect, if any effect at all, on the final form of the novel; the location of the formal divisions of the novel into parts was shifted to meet the demands of length and effect, but no part of the novel itself was moved or altered.

That portion of Book 2 taken into Book 1 in order to introduce the Vincy-Featherstone characters and prepare the readers of the parts for the absence of Dorothea (chaps. 11 and 12) ends Book 1 with Rosamond's meeting Lydgate and Fred's being asked by Peter Featherstone for a testimonial from Bulstrode. Book 2 opens with two interviews with Bulstrode: Lydgate's concerning the new hospital and the forthcoming election of chaplain, and Mr. Vincy's concerning the testimonial for Fred (chap. 13). The Lydgate and Vincy stories then alternate and cross: in chapter 14, Fred presents Bulstrode's note to Featherstone and receives money; in 15, Lydgate's past and plans are presented; in 16, Lydgate dines at the Vincy home, discusses the chaplaincy, and flirts with Rosamond; and in 17 and 18, Lydgate's moral problem concerning the vote for chaplain advances and is resolved. According to *Quarry II*, 6 and 8, Book 2 was to have ended with Fred's failure to meet his debt and his confession of that failure to Mary Garth (now in chapters 23-25). Thus the Lydgate story was to be left at his betrayal of Farebrother and Fred's story at his betrayal of the Garths. Book 3 was to open with the four chapters (then three) of Dorothea in Rome (now 19-22).

The *Quarry* indication of this earlier plan is fully confirmed by the manuscript. The last page of chapter 18 is 219, the pages dealing with Fred's failure to meet his debt are numbered 220-55, and the pages of the Dorothea chapters are numbered 256-313. The last of the Fred pages contains the now deleted note, "End of *Part II* Vol. I." The last sentence on this page, "But Fred did not go to Stone Court the next day for reasons that were quite peremptory," has been deleted and is now found as the opening sentence of chapter 26.[18] There can thus be no doubt the Fred chapters were once 19-21 and the Dorothea chapters were once 22-24, and that their positions were reversed and chapter 20 divided into 20 and 21.

There is still another difference in the sequence of chapters in this part of the novel as it was first planned and the sequence as it now stands. The Dorothea in Rome chapters, which were to have opened Book 3 and which contain pages 256-313 in the manuscript, were to have been fol-

---

[18] This is a rewritten page, half-empty, with a new series page number and without an old series one (see above, n. 14).

lowed by the chapters dealing with Casaubon's illness, Lydgate's being called in to attend Casaubon, and Mr. Brooke's invitation to Will Ladislaw (now included in chapters 28-30). This is clearly indicated in the manuscript where the page numbers in these chapters are 314-43 (see Illustration 3, Appendix A). Now, instead, these chapters are preceded by those dealing with Fred's illness and Lydgate's consequently being thrown together with Rosamond (now chapters 26 and 27), the pages of which were at one time numbered in the manuscript [346]-65. Pages 365-404 (chaps. 31-33) were to conclude Book 3, as they now do, with the engagement of Lydgate and the deathwatch over Peter Featherstone.[19]

It must be remembered that George Eliot wrote " Miss Brooke," probably the first nine-plus chapters of the novel as we now have it, as part of a story separate from that of the already begun " Middlemarch "; after she joined the two stories she interrelated the two plots and sets of characters only gradually. There are, even in the finished novel, only two meeting points of the separate stories—the transitional chapter 10 (Dorothea's pre-wedding party) and the minor part played by Mr. Brooke in the Tyke-Farebrother election (chap. 18) —until late in Book 3 (chap. 30) when Lydgate is called in to attend Casaubon. The slightness of the union is reflected in the original conception of each part as having "a certain unity & completeness in itself." Indeed, it was probably the unity and completeness of "Miss Brooke" and of the first "Middlemarch" chapters which suggested the idea of half-volumes to Lewes.

This distinctness of the early parts, each treating either a " Miss Brooke " or a " Middlemarch " subject, was first broken down by the inclusion of chapters 11 and 12, the beginning of the Lydgate-Vincy stories, in Book 1, a part significantly entitled " Miss Brooke." But even after that change it was George Eliot's intention, according to the notebook list of chapters and the pagination of the manuscript, to deal with the separate plots in long sections: to carry the Dorothea story from the opening of the novel to her marriage (nine-plus chapters); to carry the Lydgate-Vincy story to Lydgate's voting for Tyke and Fred's apparent loss of Mary Garth (eleven chapters); then to follow the Casaubons to Rome and home to Lowick until Casaubon fell ill and Will was invited to Middlemarch (seven chapters); then to bring Lydgate to the point of marriage and Peter Featherstone to the grave (eight chapters, including the first three of Book 4).

---

[19] Kitchel, p. 65, rightly observes that page 7 of *Quarry II* is a fair copy of page 8. This older page 8 confirms the existence of the earlier plan for the sequence of chapters in this part suggested by the manuscript pagination. The switch is also confirmed by the appearance of certain rewritten pages in the manuscript, e. g., the first page of chapter 31.

This plan was first changed by the moving forward of the four chapters dealing with Dorothea in Rome to follow the election of Tyke, and the moving back of Fred's failure to meet his debt and confession to Mary. The change came about not because of the " difficulty of weaving the Fred Vincy strands," which after many changes were successfully worked in " logically and naturally . . . with the Dorothea-Casaubon strand," [20] but because of the peculiar demands of the half-volume parts publication; Lewes wrote Blackwood on December 7, 1871:

By this post I send you a batch of m. s. which we should like set up in *slips* AT ONCE. We think that the absence of Dodo and her husband from Part II will be felt injuriously and that the part would be greatly strengthened in interest if some of her story be introduced, and to make way for it some scenes must be transposed to Part III. The question of how much may be transposed can't be settled until we know how much what is now sent will make.

The publisher agreed that this " change in the second part is . . . an immense improvement and makes it most attractive " (December 31, 1871). Had this change not been made, readers of the parts would have heard nothing of Dorothea for four months, from December, 1871, when Book 1 was published, until her appearance in Book 3, published in April, 1872. This would have been an impossible burden on the memory and patience of the reader. The idea of independent parts had to give way to the practical consideration of the reader of parts which were published only every other month.

Even after transposing a portion of the Dorothea plot into the " Middlemarch " Book 3, however, George Eliot wanted to keep as much of the " Middlemarch " strand in consecutive chapters as possible, and so she moved Fred's illness and the consequent Lydgate-Rosamond flirtation forward to follow Fred's apparent loss of Mary Garth, and she moved the Casaubons' return to Lowick and Mr. Casaubon's illness and its consequences back. Lydgate's attendance on Casaubon and Fred still linked the two stories, as originally intended, but the order was reversed and the " Miss Brooke " plot was broken into shorter sequences. The novel still opens with the nine-plus chapters of " Miss Brooke," but it is followed now by only eight, not eleven, " Middlemarch " chapters. There now follow four " Miss Brooke " chapters (19-22), five " Middlemarch " chapters (23-27), three more " Miss Brooke " chapters (28-30) —in the last one of which Lydgate appears as Casaubon's physician—and, bridging Books 3 and 4, six " Middlemarch " chapters (31-36) in the middle of which span, in chapter 34, a number of " Miss Brooke " characters appear at Peter Featherstone's funeral.

The original conception of the parts as distinct units had given way

---

[20] Kitchel, p. 65.

to the necessity of keeping not only elements of "Miss Brooke" and "Middlemarch" present in each part but of keeping all three plot lines—Dorothea's, Lydgate's, and Fred's—present in each part. From the end of Book 2 to near the end of the novel (Book 7) no one of the three stories is absent from a half-volume part, and no one of the stories is ever dealt with to the exclusion of the other two for more than four consecutive chapters. Even without this transposition of chapters, Lydgate would have served as a link between the Dorothea and Fred Vincy stories; perhaps all the eventual interrelationships—Dorothea-Will-Rosamond, Fred-Bulstrode-Will, etc.—would have been established without the breaking up of the plots into short sections. The unity of *Middlemarch* may be an outgrowth of the increasing interrelationship of the characters and interdependence of the plots. But the need to jump back and forth from one story to the other within the half-volume undoubtedly made George Eliot consider more carefully the relation of one story to the others and one group of characters to the others. The idea of independent parts was first broken down by the practical considerations surrounding the form of publication. The requirements of parts publication thus virtually forced George Eliot to unify *Middlemarch* in a way that she had not originally intended.

The publication of *Middlemarch* in eight half-volume parts issued over the period of a year (the last three parts were issued monthly), though it did not force George Eliot to fragment her work into small parts the length of which was controlled by publishing requirements down to the very number of lines, did force upon her attention at least three considerations not present in the publishing of a novel in book form: the lengths of the parts could not be too disparate; the ending of each part had to meet certain paradoxical requirements of continuity and completeness; and no major aspect of the novel could be omitted entirely from any one section of the novel. That the first two of these considerations caused any significant changes in the novel we cannot be sure. The last did. But the changes were beneficial rather than damaging to *Middlemarch* as a work of art.

The net effect of parts publication was, in fact, to aid George Eliot in the fusion of "Miss Brooke" and "Middlemarch" which was begun in the early chapters of the novel and continued in Books 2 and 3. But even at the end of Book 3 complete unity was not achieved and the rest of the novel did not fall neatly into place. What had to be done and what was done is the subject of the next chapter.

CHAPTER THREE

Books 4−8: From Notebook to Novel

1.

With Book 3 the basic pattern of the development of the novel was established. From that part on there is an ever-increasing interrelationship among the various strands of the story. The manuscript reveals no more dramatic changes, no more extensive shiftings of chapters or scenes. There are pages which seem to have been rewritten and pages or series of pages which seem to have been added, but there are no changes which suggest major shifts in sequence or plot. This does not mean, however, that there were no such changes; indeed, the notebook shows that George Eliot did make shifts and alterations of major proportions, but she made them before she committed the chapters and incidents concerned to paper; she made them, that is, during the planning stage.

Those plans and changes in plan which George Eliot recorded in *Quarry II* fall into two basic groups—the general, or those plans which involve the direction, development, and denouement of all that remained to be written of the entire novel at the time of the planning, and the specific, or chapter-by-chapter plans of the next part to be written— despite the many different titles given these two groups of plans in the notebook: " Motives," " Motives (in general) ," " Sketch," " Elements," " Scenes," " Course," and " Conditions."

The first of the plans appears on *Quarry II*, 9, immediately following two pages listing two different versions of the chapters which were to make up Book 3, and this first plan, called " Motives," concerns Book 4 almost exclusively. It is at this point, and with this part, Book 4, then, that the record of the planning of *Middlemarch* begins, and it is therefore here that tracing the development of these plans must begin. But before this can be done, the first half of *Quarry II* must be brought into focus.

The second flyleaf, recto and verso, which apparently begins *Quarry II*, contains lists of dates, chiefly political. It is impossible to date these lists with any certainty: they could have been written before or after page 1 or any subsequent page in *Quarry II*, or, indeed, before or after almost any portion of *Quarry I*. The list on the verso, however, because it seems to bring together many of the dates in *Quarry I*, and even those in *Quarry II*, 25, may be considered newer than the bulk of both Quarries.

The first page of *Quarry II* is headed " Queries " and lists " Periods of university examinations" and "Notes from a letter on Hospitals," the latter running over onto page 2. Information about hospitals was requested of Mrs. Richard Congreve in the autumn of 1869, but these notes refer to 1869 in terms which suggest that that year had long since passed. In fact, "Notes from a letter on Hospitals" seems to belong to the early months of 1871 when George Eliot was joining " Middlemarch " to " Miss Brooke," for following this entry on the same page of the notebook is a list of " Directors " of the new " Middlemarch " hospital which contains a " Miss Brooke " name, the name of Dorothea's uncle, " Arthur Brooke Esq. of Tipton Grange." This list of " Directors " indicates how each voted in the Tyke-Farebrother chaplaincy election which takes place in chapter 18 of the novel. Thus these entries were evidently made after the decision to join the two stories and before the completion of chapter 18, i.e., between January 1 and March 19, 1871 (see above, p. 22). This date is further confirmed by the balance of *Quarry II*, 2, which consists of a rough map containing on the one hand the town of Middlemarch and on the other such " Miss Brooke " places as Lowick, Tipton, and Freshitt. The map was drawn, surely, during the immediate post-join period when George Eliot was trying to fuse the landscapes of her two stories.

Quarry II, 3, contains a list of eleven " Relations to be developed," only the last two of which involve characters from both " Middlemarch " and " Miss Brooke." Because of the slightness of the connection between the two works which is evident in the list, and because such fundamental relationships as those of Lydgate and Rosamond to Dorothea and of Will Ladislaw to Bulstrode were omitted, this list would appear to have been drawn up very early in the post-join period, like its immediate predecessors in the notebook, probably before March 19, 1871.

The list of " Private dates " on *Quarry II*, 4, although it dates Dorothea's second marriage more than a year earlier than it takes place in the novel and gives a date for the birth of Rosamond's child, who is never born in the novel, shows to what extent George Eliot foresaw the subsequent events of the story and even their sequence, at an early stage in her writing of *Middlemarch*. The first part of this list is early; it was probably drawn up in the spring or summer of 1871: it immediately follows the list of relationships which dates from the first months of 1871, and it is immediately followed by a list of the chapters in Book 1. The latter list much postdates the idea of bimonthly publication of parts, i. e., it must be later than Lewes's letter to Blackwood suggesting the plan on May 7, 1871, since it is identified as " Part I " and dated " Decr.," the same month Book 1 of *Middlemarch* was to be published. (There is no indication that these items were added after the list had been drawn up.) On the other hand, since the subsequent list of chapters in Book 2 begins with chapter 11, the Book 1 list must be earlier than the decision to move chapters 11 and 12 back from the second to the first part, i. e., it must be earlier than Lewes's September 7, 1871, letter to Blackwood suggesting the change. The second portion of this list of private dates, which brings together the fictional events of the spring and summer of 1831 as they appear in *Middlemarch*, George Eliot must have added when she was planning these events more precisely, i. e., in the spring or early summer of 1872.[1]

It is important to recognize that the lists of chapters in the first three parts were not so much plans as they were records of accomplishment: George Eliot drew up the lists after she had completed the chapters them- selves. We know this definitely to be true of those first nine chapters written as part of the once independent " Miss Brooke." If the author made the list of directors and their votes on page 2 while she was writing chapter 18, we can be sure that she had completed at least eighteen chap- ters before making up the lists. Each chapter in the first two parts is followed in these lists by an accurate record of the manuscript pages it contains, so that unless George Eliot added these numbers later—and there is no evidence of this—they indicate that she had completed at least the first two parts before making up the notebook lists. The lists of the chapters in Book 3 contain no manuscript page numbers; that there are two differing lists of the chapters in Book 3 indicates that the part had not reached its present form when the earlier of these lists had been made. But the pagination of the manuscript adheres to the sequence of the earlier plan, indicating that the manuscript could have been written even before the earlier list was drawn up and certainly was written before the later list was; that there are no other plans for Book 3 in the notebook also suggests that the part had been written first and then the notebook entries made.

On *Quarry II*, 9, there is a list of " Motives," which, for the most part, involves the matter of Book 4. On the next page is a list of the chapters in Book 4. On page 11 is a list of " Motives (in general) ," which includes

---

[1] The list of private dates is as follows, with punctuation altered for clarity: " Dorothea married, 1827 [*sic*]. Featherstone dies & Ladislaw comes to Tipton, Ap. 1830. Celia married May. Lydgate's marriage 1830—July or August. Mr. Brooke tries for Parliament, May 1831. Mr. Casaubon's death, 1831, March. Celia's baby born, 1831, April. Dorothea's second marriage, 1832, Jan. or Feb. Child born, 1833. Rosa- mond's baby born, June 1, 1831. Bulstrode buys Stone Court, June or July 1831. Raffles comes back, July 1831. Raffles dies, Aug. 1832, two years after Lydgate's

details for Book 5 and for subsequent parts, followed on the same page by a list headed "Continuation of Part V." On page 12 is a list of the chapters in Book 5. George Eliot, it seems, either planned a part, wrote it, and recorded the chapters in her notebook; or she planned a part, planned the sequence of chapters in the part and recorded it in her notebook, and then wrote the part. The former is the more likely hypothesis, as analysis of the notebook plans will show.

The next notebook pages, 13-15, contain the *final* lists of chapters for Books 6-8. George Eliot, knowing there were to be eight parts, apparently just left three notebook pages blank after the list of chapters in Book 5 and completed the part-by-part lists of chapters after she had written each of the parts. These lists were thus records of accomplishment, not sketches or plans of material yet to be written. This is confirmed by much of the material which makes up the rest of *Quarry II* following these lists; e. g., the list of "Elements of B. VI" on page 26 was obviously a rough plan for that part written long before George Eliot determined the actual forms, subjects, and sequences implied by the chapters listed for that part on page 13.[2]

The chapter-by-chapter list for each part on pages 5, 6, 7, 10, and 12-15 in *Quarry II* were recorded just before, during, or just after the chapters or parts themselves were written and must be considered the *final* notebook entries for those parts. All other material in the notebook relative to those parts must be considered earlier plans or steps along the way toward the completion of the chapters there listed. It is only with this chronology firmly established that any analysis of the planning and writing of the parts can be made. The balance of this chapter will be devoted to such an analysis.

marriage." What has been identified as the later list continues after a space with a second mention of Casaubon's death: "Mr. Casaubon's death, March 1831. Dorothea settled at Lowick again, June 1831. Bulstrode & Raffles at Stone Court, end of June 1831. Fred Vincy's adventure & choice, July 1831. Lydgate's disclosure of trouble to Rosd., Aug."

[2] Miss Kitchel is led into many errors by not suspecting that the chapter-by-chapter lists of the parts on these earlier pages were not in fact written after the pages which by their numbers seem to be later. For example, she considers (p. 17) the "Scenes" on *Quarry II*, 29-30, to be "developed with much more psychological and dramatic detail" than are "the outlines of Parts VII and VIII on pages 14 and 15," and calls those scenes closer to the final form; but not only do these scenes refer to Books 6 and 8 rather than 7 and 8, but they also have Dorothea's second marriage occurring before the Bulstrode-Lydgate-Raffles scandal, whereas in both the lists on pages 14-15 and in the novel this order is reversed. In the list of scenes on pages 29-30 Dorothea tells Sir James of her decision to marry Will; in the novel, as in the list on page 15, it is Mr. Brooke who carries the news. There can be no doubt that the lists on pages 14-15 are later than the list of "Scenes" on pages 29-30. For a detailed treatment of Books 6-8 as they are developed in the notebook and the novel, see sections 5-7 in this chapter.

2.

Though George Eliot finished writing Book 3 by October 29, 1871, she continued to fuss with it while she worked on Book 4, not making the transpositions of chapters discussed above until at least December 7, 1871. On December 1, when Book 1 was published, she was concerned about her slow pace: " I ought by this time to have finished the fourth part, but an illness . . . has robbed me of two months " (*Life* 3: 144). It was no wonder she was concerned: thirteen months had now passed since she had begun " Miss Brooke," and if the scheme of bimonthly publication were to be adhered to, only fourteen months remained in which to write the rest of the novel. Almost three weeks later, on December 20, she was " only at p. 227 of my fourth part. But I have been retarded by construction, which, once done, serves as good wheels for progress." [3] On January 18, 1872, George Eliot wrote Blackwood implying that Book 4 was finished—" Mr. Lewes is much satisfied with the Fourth Book "—but she recorded in her journal on January 29, "I have finished the fourth part—*i. e.*, the second volume—of ' Middlemarch' " (*Life* 3: 150), which seems to imply " just finished." Since chapter 42 is numbered as if it were intended to open a new part but is in fact the closing chapter of Book 4, it was probably chapter 41 which George Eliot finished on January 18 and chapter 42 which she completed on January 29.

Thus George Eliot wrote Book 4 in three months, a month faster than she had completed Book 3, but at a pace which would scarcely keep her up with the printers if bimonthly parts were to appear. But she hoped that the work on construction which had here slowed her pace would speed the writing of the later parts (as indeed it did). It is these plans for construction, beginning with page 9 of *Quarry II*—the nature and origins of which have just been discussed—and it is the earlier of these plans, those dealing with the events of Book 4, that will here be traced from the notebook into the novel.

Book 3 contained Fred's failure to meet his debt, his confession of that failure to the Garths, his falling ill, and his treatment by Lydgate.

---

[3] *Life* 3: 145. There are two pages 227 in MS. 2. The first (Cabinet Edition 2: 155) begins with the salutation of Will's reply to Casaubon's letter and was meant to follow immediately after Will's receipt of that letter on page 226. George Eliot renumbered the page 234. The second page 227 (Cabinet Edition 2: 148) immediately follows the signature " Edward Casaubon," George Eliot apparently having added the seven intervening pages in revision.

N. B., this is page 227 of the second volume, *not* the 227th page of Book 4. The part begins on page 151; thus George Eliot had written just 77 of the 164 manuscript pages which now make up the part, or four of the nine chapters, and had finished less than half the part.

During Fred's illness Rosamond and Lydgate had an unprecedented opportunity to see each other alone and to continue what was to Lydgate their flirtation. In the midst of this flirtation Lydgate was called to the Casaubons. Mr. Casaubon had had a heart attack occasioned by a letter from Will Ladislaw. The letter from Will was answered by Mr. Brooke with an invitation to visit him at Tipton. Lydgate, meanwhile, was engaged to Rosamond, and Featherstone was dying surrounded by his greedy relatives. Peter Featherstone's death in the middle of the night, with Mary Garth attending, ends the part.

Book 3 contains chapters 23-33, manuscript pages 220-56, [346]-365, 314-44, and another 365-404. Book 4, called "Three Love Problems," begins with chapter 34, manuscript page 405 (151 n. s.), runs to page 296 n. s., and from 1 (or "x") of a third series of numbers through page 18, i. e., through chapter 42. According to George Eliot's descriptions of the chapters in this part in the notebook (but not according to her numbering of these chapters, which is erroneous because chapters 20-21 were still one chapter), Book 4 consists of the following:

34 Featherstone buried & Ladislaw resuscitated
35 The Reading of the Will.
36 Lydgate and Rosamond advance toward marriage
37 Ladislaw's settlement at Middlemarch, in relation to Dorothea & Mr. Casaubon
38 Sir James & the Cadwalladers attack Mr. Brooke about the management of the farms
39 Dorothea goes to the Grange, & Dagley has his say
40 Caleb Garth at breakfast etc.
41 Mr. Raffles visits Mr. Rigg
42 Mr. Casaubon in prospect of death

The integrating of all elements in the novel into each part, which began with the extending of Book 1 to include chapters 11 and 12 and continued with the transposing of chapters 23-25 and 19-22 and of chapters 28-30 and 26-27 in Books 2 and 3, continued still further in this part though no such changes were necessary. The part opens with Featherstone's funeral, a scene in which all the characters from all parts of the plot are on stage and in which the "Miss Brooke" plot is furthered in this ostensibly "Middlemarch" chapter by the reappearance of Will Ladislaw on the Middlemarch scene. The reading of the will (chap. 35) concerns chiefly the Fred-Mary third of the plot, but the surprise heir of Stone Court, Joshua Rigg, is soon to be connected with Bulstrode and thus with Lydgate, and eventually with Will Ladislaw. Mr. Vincy's disappointment in the Featherstone will serves as a transition from the affairs of Fred to those of his sister Rosamond in the third chapter (36) of this part; his vexation results not in an end to her engagement to Lydgate but in an earlier wedding. Mr. Vincy sees his worsening family affairs as part of the general upheaval of the times, which observation leads the reader to the political scene and to Will Ladislaw. The next three chapters (37-39) concern Will and politics and Will and Dorothea. The seventh chapter (40) of the part moves from the Brookes back to the Garths: Mr. Brooke has been attacked by the opposition press for the manner in which he conducts his own estate and decides to place the estate in the hands of Caleb Garth. The Garths are thus on their way back to more prosperous times after the strain of having had to pay Fred's debt. Caleb's prosperity is further insured by Mr. Bulstrode's asking him to assess Stone Court, which the banker intends buying from Rigg. The two commissions link "Miss Brooke" to "Middlemarch" through Caleb Garth.[4] The next to last chapter (41) of the part concerns Rigg and introduces his stepfather, Raffles, who is to play so large a part in the denouement of the novel. Chapter 41 was to have ended Book 4—the wheel has gone full circle in this part, from Rigg back to Rigg—but another chapter (42) was added, carrying the story back once again to Casaubon and to Lydgate, now married, who is attending him. Chapter 42 still bears the marks of an opening chapter: it is the first chapter in this section not linked to the one before it, and its first sentence sounds like a new beginning—"One of the professional calls made by Lydgate soon after his return from his wedding journey. . . ."

The only plan for Book 4 in the *Quarry* is the list of "Motives" on page 9, and this list is well advanced toward the final shape of the part. The first item—"Featherstone's burial. Arrival of Ladislaw"—though worded somewhat differently, is essentially the same as George Eliot's title of the first chapter of the part. The second item—"Will read, & Family consternation"—is simply a fuller statement of the title of the second chapter of the part, chapter 35. Earlier statements and plans in the *Quarry* are usually more detailed than the chapter-title lists. George Eliot attempted in these earlier notes to clarify incidents and situations for her own benefit, but in the chapter-title lists simply noted completed work as briefly as possible for her own reference. The third item— "Advent of the new stranger, Rigg"—may be out of order, Rigg having been noticed during the reading of the will, though his "advent" is part of this same chapter. The fourth item—"Lydgate & Rosamond married"— is only indirectly included in Book 4: chapter 36 shows the wedding date being moved forward; chapter 42 indicates that Lydgate has already been married and has now returned from his honeymoon. It is possible that

---

[4] See item 10 of the "Relations to be developed," *Quarry II*, 3: "of Caleb Garth to Mr. Brooke etc."

at the time she made up this list of "Motives" George Eliot did not foresee that she would write chapter 36, i. e., that she would link the speeding-up of the marriage to Fred's not having inherited Stone Court. The fifth item in the list—"Mr. Brooke seen to be making political tentatives. Ladislaw's relation to Dorothea & Mr. Casaubon shown, a propos of appointment to edit the Pioneer"—is again a fuller statement of the title of chapter 37. The sixth and seventh items—"Dismay of Sir James & the Cadwalladers" and "Attacks on Mr. Brooke as a Landlord"—are both included in chapter 38. There is no suggestion in the list, however, of chapter 39, in which Dorothea visits the Grange and Brooke visits Dagley; this "unscheduled" chapter furthers somewhat the Will-Dorothea relationship, but the function of the Dagley episode is not immediately apparent. The eighth item in the list of "Motives"—"He [Mr. Brooke] is induced to give management of his estate to Caleb Garth"—is presented in the novel, chapter 40, from the point of view of Garth and serves as a transition from the Brooke to the Garth, and thence to the Bulstrode, plot lines. According to the list of "Motives," the Garth story was to have been continued, and it was apparently to have been at this point that Fred was to go to work for Mr. Garth, for the ninth item in the list is "What Fred Vincy does"; in the novel this is no longer the case. The tenth item—"How Lydgate goes on medically, & in relation to Bulstrode & the Hospital"—also does not appear in Book 4 of the novel, and after this item in the list George Eliot wrote "vide P. V," apparently when she saw that this situation would have to wait at least until the next part for development. The eleventh and last item—"Looming of Raffles"—is the subject of the next to last chapter of Book 4, chapter 41, but again the author apparently had not seen how she was to move from one portion of the plot to the other; this subject in the novel is very smoothly introduced via Caleb Garth, who is commissioned by Bulstrode to go to Stone Court, there sees Raffles, etc., no hint of which was given in the list.

In short, then, all of the chapters in Book 4 except chapters 39-42 (the last not originally intended to appear in this part anyway) are specifically mentioned in this list of "Motives," and all of the "Motives" but two form chapters or portions of chapters in this part, these two appearing in later parts. The sequence, too, of this list of "Motives," except perhaps for the "Advent of . . . Rigg" following the reading of the will, is an accurate picture of the sequence of events in Book 4. Thus the only planning of this part which appears in the notebook shows that Book 4 was rather fully developed in the author's mind before she began writing it. The only aspect of any significance which was improved upon or changed in any way, other than the postponement of Fred's choice of a career and a summary of Lydgate's progress or situation, is the transition between the various strands of the plot, which, almost absent from the list of "Motives," is quite clear in the list of chapters in this part and even clearer in the novel itself.

3.

Two days after George Eliot finished Book 4, Book 2 was published. Two months later, April, 1872, when Book 3 appeared, she had not yet finished Book 5. On April 29, John Blackwood announced his intention of coming to London on May 8 on his way to the Continent and hinted gently, perhaps, that she was falling behind in her writing—"When are we to get any more M.S.? " Exactly on May 8, according to her journal, she finished Book 5 (*Life* 3: 158) .[5] If this date is correct, it had taken George Eliot about the same amount of time to write Book 5 as it had to write Book 4, about three months. At this rate she would not be able to meet the scheduled bimonthly publication of the parts.

The construction which was to pave the way for more rapid writing of the latter half of the novel had not yet yielded this advantage. The notebook from here on, however, shows, for the first time, signs of planning and of changes of plan. Here we can begin to trace George Eliot's creative method.

The chapters of Book 5 (with chapter 42, which had been moved back into Book 4, omitted) were listed on *Quarry II*, 12, as follows:

43 Dorothea goes into Middlemarch: calls at Lydgate's
44 Dorothea & Lydgate talk of the Hospital
45 Lydgate's medical position: scene between him & Rosamond.
46 Mr. Brooke & Ladislaw. Lydgate & Ladislaw.
47 Will goes to Lowick Church
48 Mr. Casaubon's last wishes
    Mr. Casaubon dies
49 Sir James & Mr. Brooke confer about the Will
50 Celia "prepares" Dorothea, & Lydgate exerts his influence for Mr. Farebrother.
51 Mr. Brooke addresses the electors.
52 Mr. Farebrother performs a difficult duty.
53 Raffles reappears

In Book 5, even more than in Book 4, the integration of the three

---

[5] Professor Haight found the text of a letter from George Eliot to Simpson, printed in a Maggs Brothers catalogue and dated there April 6, 1872, which announced the mailing of the manuscript of Book 5 and of a list of errata for Book 4. If these are proof corrections for Book 4, due to be published in June, 1872, April 6 would seem a bit early for this letter to have been written. In any case, the May 8 journal entry and Blackwood's query about the manuscript suggest that the date ascribed to the letter in the catalogue may be in error.

major strands of the novel into each part may be seen. Here not only are all three major strands present, but they no longer appear as separate strands. Friendship has sprung up between Dorothea and her husband's physician, Lydgate; Rosamond is engaged in a mild flirtation with Will Ladislaw, and Mr. Farebrother, for whom Lydgate intercedes with Dorothea, is himself the intercessor for Fred Vincy with Mary Garth.[6] Not only are the Vincy and Lydgate strands of " Middlemarch " interwoven, but there no longer seem to be " Miss Brooke " and " Middlemarch " halves to the novel.

The above chapter list was, of course, written late, probably after the chapters themselves were complete. Except for the item marked " vide P.V " in the list of " Motives " discussed in the previous section of this chapter, the first list in *Quarry II* having to do with this part appears on page 11 and is headed " Motives (in general) ." Of the dozen items in this list only from two to four refer directly to Book 5; the others, as perhaps signified by the parenthetical " in general," refer to all the rest of the novel. Those items which definitely apply to Book 5 are the first two—" Mr. Casaubon dies " and " Mr. Brooke stands and falls "—which appear in chapters 48 and 51 respectively. The fourth item—" Raffles comes on the scene "—may refer to his first appearance in chapter 41, Book 4, or to his reappearance in chapter 53, Book 5. Similarly, the tenth item in this list—" Rosamond's flirtation with Ladislaw "—may refer to chapter 43, Book 5, but more probably refers to chapter 77, Book 8, especially since in this list it follows " Blight on Bulstrode & Lydgate " and is followed by " Dorothea after severe struggles goes to Rosamond," both incidents from Book 8.

Immediately following this list of " Motives (in general) " in the notebook are five items headed " Continuation of Part V." The first—" About Mr. Farebrother's appointment to Lowick "—apparently refers to Lydgate's conversation with Dorothea about that appointment in chapter 50. The second item—" Mr. Brooke goes to the hustings "—refers to the next chapter, chapter 51. The third item—" Fred Vincy's choice of career "—like the item in the preceding list of " Motives "—" What Fred Vincy does "—was postponed, not appearing at all in Book 5. The fourth item in this later list was queried by the author—" Raffles' return? "—but it appears as the last chapter in this part, chapter 53; the question mark may not have questioned the incident itself but whether it was to have appeared in this part or in the next. The last item in " Continuation of Part V "—" Drama of Will & Dorothea advanced "—is sufficiently general to cause doubt: does it refer to Will's visit to Lowick Church (chapter 47) or to

---

[6] See *Quarry II*, 3, " Relations to be developed ": " 11 of Mr Farebrother to all, except Sir J. & Mr Brooke."

the " Interview & goodbye between Dorothea & Will " which opens Book 6, chapter 54? Because these items are more or less in the sequence in which they appear in the novel, and because the item preceding this one, Raffles' return, appears in the last chapter of Book 5, it is more likely that this entry refers to the first chapter in Book 6, chapter 54.

It is apparent already that these two lists on *Quarry II*, 11, reflect less accurately the contents and sequence of events in Book 5 than the list of " Motives " did those in Book 4. In the list for Book 4, each item, or at most two items, appeared as a chapter in the novel, and chapter followed chapter much as item followed item, except for two of the last three entries in the list. In the list for Books 5 *et seq.* the first item, regarding Casaubon's death, is the sixth chapter in Book 5, and the second item, Brooke's standing and falling, is the ninth of the eleven chapters of this part. Of the remaining ten items in this general list only one, or at most two, appear in Book 5. Even in the list marked " Continuation of Part V," though the sequence is similar to that of the events in the novel, only three of the five items listed actually appear in Book 5.

There are lists much later in *Quarry II* which also contain items relative to Book 5 of *Middlemarch*. The first such list, on page 23, is unheaded and contains but five items:

> How Ladislaw goes on in Middlemarch
> Initiates relation to Rosamond
> Scene of Fred Vincy's choice, after Mar. 31
> Ladislaw's birth known
> Mr. Farebrother's appointment to the living.

The first of these items undoubtedly refers to chapter 46, called in the chapter list of Book 5, " Mr. Brooke & Ladislaw. Lydgate & Ladislaw," but which in fact presents Will's progress in Middlemarch and the attitude of the Middlemarchers toward him. The second item also apparently refers to that chapter, though Will had been alone with Rosamond as early as chapter 43. The third and fourth items appear in Book 6. The last, which occurs during Book 5, takes place off stage: Lydgate interceded for Farebrother with Dorothea in chapter 50; chapter 52 begins, " On that June evening when Mr. Farebrother knew that he was to have the Lowick living . . ." (2: 360) .

This short list on page 23 should be viewed in the light of page 11. On page 11, under " Motives (in general) ," the two major *events* of Book 5, both of which affect Ladislaw, were recorded—Casaubon's death and Brooke's political failure. The first two items in this later list sketch the situation of Ladislaw in Middlemarch within which these effects will operate, ending one phase of his Middlemarch experience, as Brooke's political adviser, and beginning another, as Rosamond's courtier. The

"Motives (in general)" list, because it concerns itself simply with the chief events, would seem earlier than the unheaded list on page 23 which situates those events. But the list called "Continuation of Part V" on page 11 would seem later than the unheaded list on page 23 since its ordering of events more nearly predicts the sequence of events in the novel.

On page 24 there is a list of twelve numbered items headed "Elements." A little more than the first half of this list pertains to Book 5. The first item—"Mr. Casaubon makes arrangements about his will, having been stimulated by Lydgate's answers to his inquiries about his health"—refers rather clearly to chapter 42, although the arrangements are made off stage and are brought to light only after Casaubon's death (chap. 49); as has been mentioned, chapter 42, which was to have been the first chapter of Book 5, was moved back to become the last of Book 4. The second item in the list—"Lydgate again in colloquy with Dorothea, whence an occasion for her to apply some money"—refers to the next chapter but one, chapter 44, the intervening chapter having to do with Dorothea's visit to Lydgate's house and discovery of Will Ladislaw there. The third item—"Collision between Lydgate & medical men connected with Bulstrode"—is presented in the next chapter, 45. The fourth item— "Leading up to Mr. Brooke's nomination in *April or May* 1831; his failure & loss of appetite for a public career"—was divided into two parts by the semicolon, the second part marked in the notebook, "β." The first part of this appears in the first half of chapter 46, "Mr. Brooke & Ladislaw. Lydgate & Ladislaw"; the second half does not appear until chapter 51.[7] The fifth item—"Mr. Casaubon's death. Sir James & Celia"— is again made up of two parts, this time separated by a period. The first appears in chapter 48; the second, insofar as Sir James is involved, forms part of chapter 49, and, insofar as Celia is involved, part of chapter 50. The sixth item—"Fred Vincy's debate about his career"—at first seems to concern the scene of his choice of career, once before delayed, but it more than likely refers to his internal debate and the revelation of that debate to Mr. Farebrother, now in chapter 52. The last item which has

---

[7] What separates the two elements of this item in the novel are Will's visit to Lowick Church and Casaubon's death. The reason for the separation seems evident. On *Quarry II*, 27, in a summary of the events of this plot line called "*Will Ladislaw & Dorothea*," the first sentence says, "An offence springs up between Mr. Brooke & Will." The offence is necessary to rupture the close relationship between the two men; in the novel it takes the form of the codicil to Casaubon's will which makes it impossible for Brooke to continue to employ the man of whom his niece's husband was jealous. Thus Will's offending Casaubon by his visit to the church, Casaubon's death, and the codicil had to intervene between the preparation for Brooke's campaign in chapter 46 and his failure, in chapter 51, which gives him an excuse to sever his relations with Will, the real reason being the codicil.

to do with Book 5, No. 7—" Arrival of Raffles "—is, for some reason I have not been able to ascertain, marked " δ." [8] This return of Raffles was listed in the " Continuation of Part V " with a question mark but does find its way into the part as the last chapter, 53.

The list of " Elements," then, presents items of Book 5 more or less in the order in which they appear in the novel, though the division into chapters was still not too clear. Since the list continues for five more items beyond the last one applicable to Book 5, it is obvious that the ending of this part was not yet definite at the time the list of " Elements " was made. This list begins with the subject matter of the last chapter (42) of Book 4. We know from the manuscript pagination that George Eliot decided about the time she finished writing chapter 45 not to open Book 5 with this chapter. Therefore we can with some certainty date the list as earlier than the completion of chapter 45. The list of " Elements " seems about as accurate and about as close to the final version of this part of the novel as is " Continuation of Part V," and thus they probably belong to about the same stage of the planning, though the " Continuation," because it includes " Fred Vincy's choice of a career," and not, like " Elements " and like the novel, his " debate " about his career, is probably slightly the earlier.

The only notebook entries having to do with Book 4 were found to be extremely close to the final scope and sequence of the chapters as they appear in that part of the novel. The notebook entries involving details of Book 5 are both more numerous and more diverse. The first plan, " Motives (in general)," includes details from all the last parts of the novel, only two of which are clearly pertinent to Book 5, but these items are, in fact, the two chief " incidents " of the part. The unheaded list on *Quarry II*, 23, presents only Will Ladislaw's situation, providing a sort of setting for the main events of Book 5, but it also contains, along with the third most important " incident "—Farebrother's receiving the Lowick living—two items which are not included in this part at all. The list called " Continuation of Part V," which was apparently added to the " Motives (in general) " list on page 11, includes one of these two items,

---

[8] The order in " Elements " is: (1) Brooke's political failure, (2) Casaubon's death, (3) Fred's debate, and (4) Raffles' arrival. The desired order eventually, according to the final version in the novel, is 2, 1, 3, 4. Perhaps, then, Brooke's failure was marked *beta* to show that it was to come after Casaubon's death and Raffles' arrival was marked *delta* to show that it was still fourth, with the *alpha* and *gamma* of Casaubon's death and Fred's debate not marked down but understood. Item 10— " Lydgate attends Raffles' death-bed "—is marked *epsilon*, probably to show it is to precede item 9—" Second marriage of Dorothea "—though it does not precede item 8— " Embarrassments of Lydgate."

Fred's choice of a career, which does not appear in Book 5, but much more nearly reflects the actual chapter sequence of the last portion of Book 5. The list of "Elements" on *Quarry II*, 24, would seem to represent the last prewriting stage of planning in the notebook. Here four of the first five chapters (according to the initial plan of beginning the part with chapter 42) are faithfully presented in the first three and one-half items of the list, the seventh and eighth chapters of Book 5 are presented in item 5 of the list, and two of the next three chapters in the next two items on the list (the third of these chapters having been included in item 4).

The process is clear. George Eliot first noted the big incidents of a part, i. e., "what happens." She then concerned herself with the effects of the events on one or more characters, filling in necessary details of their recent histories to bring these effects into focus. These details in turn suggested other necessities or relationships which serve as links or transitions. An example of how such unpremeditated relationships enrich the novel is evident in the progress toward the completion of Book 5. It was necessary to have Mr. Brooke and Ladislaw end their relationship. This was to be done in part by Brooke's failure in his standing for Parliament, but that was not enough; some "offence" had to spring up between them. With Brooke's failure, the most important event in the part is the death of Casaubon. His death, via a codicil to his will, was made to serve as the basis for the "offence"; Brooke has to dissociate himself from Will because of the relationship between Brooke's niece Dorothea and Will which was implied in Casaubon's will. There is no evidence in the notebook that George Eliot foresaw this integration of the events of Book 5 before she began writing the part itself. There is no hint of Casaubon's will in the list of "Motives (in general)" or in the list called "Continuation of Part V." "Elements" mentions no will but simply notes after Casaubon's death, "Sir James & Celia." Thus the relationships among characters and incidents in the part grow in complexity and richness, and the outlines or "ideas" with which George Eliot began assume new shapes; the result is almost invariably longer, not shorter, than the plan. For this reason, she can have no very accurate idea of precisely what portion of the story will fit into each part. The lists of "Motives (in general)" and "Elements" give no indication of how many parts were envisioned or of how much of the story was to unfold in each. This exfoliation continued up to and through the actual writing of the chapters themselves. Only after George Eliot had written them could she draw up the final chapter-by-chapter lists of each part, such as those on pages 5-7, 10, and 12-15.

4.

The move to Elversley, Redhill, late in May, just before publication of Book 4 of *Middlemarch*, was good for the health of the novelist and for the progress of her novel. She finished Book 6 before John Blackwood returned from the Continent, less than two months after finishing Book 5; on July 2, 1872, Lewes wrote William Blackwood announcing the mailing of the manuscript of Book 6.[9] Indeed, Lewes was so encouraged by the novel's progress that on July 13, 1872, in a letter welcoming John Blackwood home, he proposed that the last two parts be published at monthly rather than bimonthly intervals, which proposal was carried out, and spoke in unusually optimistic tones about the novelist's health.

The more quickly George Eliot wrote, it seems, the more numerous were her notebook plans. Certainly her plans for Book 6 in the notebook are more extensive than those for any previous part.

Book 6 contains manuscript pages x-149 in a fifth series of page numbers, George Eliot now paginating by parts. Inserted pages numbered 17a, 40a, 96a, and 130a-f bring the actual total of manuscript pages in this part to 158. In her notebook George Eliot recorded the total as 156, apparently having taken into account some but not all the additions (further evidence, incidentally, that she was paying attention to the length of her serial parts but not tailoring them to any very exact measure).

In all, there are nine chapters in Book 6, designated on *Quarry II*, 13, as follows:

> 54 Interview & goodbye between Dorothea & Will
> 55 Dorothea declares she shall not remarry
> 56 Fred Vincy chooses his vocation.
> 58[10] Lydgate embarrassed. Scene with R.
> 57 Fred Vincy becomes jealous.
> 59 Rosamond tells Will about the codicil
> 60 The Sale. Raffles recognizes Will
> 61 Interview between Will & Bulstrode.
> 62 Interview between Will & Dorothea.

[9] She finished the part a few days earlier. Haight, in n. 6 to a letter dated June 30, 1872, indicates that Lewes had gone to Weybridge for the weekend " while GE began Book VII of *Middlemarch*."

[10] Chapter numbers are those of published text. George Eliot switched chapters 57 and 58 *after* she wrote them: the manuscript pages of chapter 57 were numbered 81-94 and the pages of chapter 58 were 53-80 before she revised and renumbered; notebook chapter numbers follow original sequence.

The switch apparently was to reduce the number of shifts from one thread of the story to the other. Originally the first two chapters dealt with Dorothea, the next with Fred, the next with Lydgate, the next with Fred, the next with Lydgate (via Rosamond) and Dorothea (via Will). Now the first two chapters deal with Dorothea,

Plans for the various incidents and chapters vary so greatly that it is convenient at first to discuss the planning of this part of the novel, not according to the sequence of these events in the part nor even according to the sequence in some one list in the notebook, but rather in the order of the first appearance of these incidents in the notebook.

The first incident from this part to appear in the notebook is Fred's choice of a career. It was apparently introduced, under the heading "What Fred does," as early as the list of "Motives" on *Quarry II*, 9, most of which appeared in Book 4. It was the third item in the "Continuation of Part V" list on *Quarry II*, 11. It was again the third item in the unheaded list on page 23, three of the five items of which appeared in Book 5. Fred finally does make his choice in the third chapter of this part, though in the list of "Elements of B. VI" on *Quarry II*, 6, his choice is the last of the seven items listed.

The financial embarrassment of Lydgate has a somewhat similar history. It first appeared as the third of the "Motives (in general)" on page 11—"Embarrassment of Lydgate" (the first two and fourth of the "Motives"—"Mr. Casaubon dies," "Mr. Brooke stands & falls," and "Raffles comes on the scene" appeared in Book 5). It then appeared as the eighth of the "Elements" on page 24, the first seven of which appeared in Book 5 also. It was expanded in the list of "Elements of B. VI" on page 26: "Lydgate gets more embarrassed, & moody in consequence/ Rosamond makes him angry by writing to his uncle." Finally, it appeared as the fifth item in the list of twenty-three "Scenes" on pages 29-30, a list which apparently was drawn up late in the planning of this portion of the novel. Here Lydgate's reactions were more concrete and detailed: "Lydgate embarrassed more & more, is moody. Rosamond, discontented, writes to Sir Godwin. Sir Godwin replies to Lydgate. His anger with R." The details after the first sentence of this note apply more directly to Book 7 of *Middlemarch* but at this time evidently were intended for Book 6 since they follow Fred's seeking "employment with Mr. Garth" and are followed in turn by six other items which appear in Book 6.

The notebook thus reveals how Lydgate's financial troubles grew more concrete as the planning of this portion of the novel progressed, grew from a "motif" to a series of "scenes." Even in the "Scenes," however, there is no indication that the troubles are to be so detailed as to involve four chapters, as they now do in the novel, three of which open Book 7.

the next two with Fred, the next two with Lydgate. George Eliot had gone from one extreme—individual half-volume parts devoted to one plot line—to the other—shifting from one of the three main story lines to another after each chapter. With this revision, she attempted to strike a balance between isolated story blocks and mixed story fragments.

The first of the Book 7 chapters, in which Farebrother offers Lydgate help and is refused (chap. 63), is nowhere hinted at in the notebook plans, though the two subsequent chapters concern the letters to and from Sir Godwin mentioned in the "Scenes" summary. Even in the chapter in Book 6 in which Lydgate finally discloses his trouble to Rosamond, the central chapter in this portion of the plot (chap. 58), George Eliot filled in details which she apparently had not foreseen when she was making her notebook plans, the details of Rosamond's miscarriage. In the list of "Private dates" on *Quarry II*, 4, one item states, "Rosamond's baby born, June 1, 1831." There are no further items dealing with the baby and nothing in the notebook to show how or when George Eliot changed her mind, but in *Middlemarch* Rosamond's baby is never born. Several months before Lydgate tells his wife of their financial difficulties, as chapter 58 explains, Rosamond, willful and vain, had ridden out with one of Lydgate's relatives, a captain, who was visiting them, and, despite her husband's warning, had ridden out a second time. This time the horse shied and she lost her baby. After her miscarriage Rosamond was ill for several months, so that during that period Lydgate did not tell her about the mounting financial problem.

The rest of Book 6, and the largest portion of that part, has to do with Will Ladislaw, his relations with Dorothea, with Rosamond, and with Bulstrode, and may be discussed more or less in the order in which these relationships develop in the novel.

The opening chapter of Book 6 deals with Will's first farewell, the second chapter with Dorothea's consequent announcement that she will not marry a second time (chaps. 54-55). It is this situation, perhaps, which was referred to in *Quarry II*, 11, as part of the "Continuation of Part V": "Drama of Will & Dorothea advanced." This aspect of the plot is absent from the list of "Elements" on page 24, though the ninth item in that list, following Lydgate's embarrassment and preceding Raffles' death, is the premature announcement, "Second marriage of Dorothea," which event, as we shall see, was to have taken place earlier in the novel than is now the case. In the list of "Elements of B. VI" on page 26, however, the farewell scene is, as it is in the novel, first— "First meeting between Will & Dorothea after her husband's death." In the list of "Scenes" on pages 29-30 it occupies the same position— "1. First interview between Will & Dorothea after her husband's death"— in this case followed, as in the novel, by "2. Dorothea tells Sir James & Celia that she will not marry again. Entertaining projects of usefulness." These "projects of usefulness," which threaten the reader with thunderous echoes of the latter stages of *Romola*, are first mentioned in

Quarry II, 27, in a summary of the Will-Dorothea plot for the last three parts of *Middlemarch* which begins:

Will Ladislaw & Dorothea

An offence springs up between Mr. Brooke & Will. Will, going on as editor of the *Pioneer*, comes to Lowick to see the Farebrothers, & has an interview with Dorothea. They part with a sense of being divided by destiny.

Dorothea has projects about filling her life: tells Sir James & Celia that she will never be married again—Celia's boy will have everything. She will go on some heroic errand of carrying away emigrants etc. Meanwhile the cholera. . . .

The "offence" has been discussed earlier in this chapter. The rest of the first paragraph of this summary is embodied in chapter 54, though in somewhat different form: there is no mention of Will's continuing with the *Pioneer*; Dorothea wants to meet Will at the Farebrothers' but the meeting does not occur there, Will finally coming to Lowick Manor to say goodbye. The projects, in chapter 55, after Dorothea has announced her intention not to remarry, are as noble as those in the summary:

". . . I have delightful plans. I should like to take a great deal of land, and drain it, and make a little colony, where everybody should work, and all the work should be done well. I should know every one of the people and be their friend. I am going to have great consultations with Mr. Garth: he can tell me almost everything I want to know" (3: 26-27).

These plans are reminiscent of those of Trawley, the mutual friend of Farebrother and Lydgate, who was going to go "to the Backwoods to found a sort of Pythagorean community" but set up practice at a German spa instead—a foreshadowing of Lydgate's fate—and married a rich patient, just as Rosamond will marry a rich physician after Lydgate's early death—and are like Will Ladislaw's later plans of colonization (3: 339) which also come to nothing. The fact that the author knows and the reader strongly suspects that the plans will never be carried out, and the lofty adjectives used, "*delightful* plans," "*great* consultations," cast an ironic glimmer over the passage, an irony similar to that of Dorothea's earlier disappointment that the good living conditions of the Lowick farmers left her no noble work to do. The threat of cholera never materializes.

The "Elements of B. VI" outline the continuation of the Will-Dorothea plot in this manner: "Will & Dorothea meet again & part with a sense that they can't marry, Will knowing all./ Rosamond flirting with Will." On the next page of the notebook, the "*Will Ladislaw & Dorothea*" narrative summary continues from the threat of cholera quoted above:

Will does not go away & gets more intimate with Mrs. Lydgate. Learns the nature of Mr. Casaubon's codicil; also about his mother's family from Bulstrode. There is another meeting & parting between him & Dorothea. . . .

Three of the " Scenes " on page 29 restate this development:

   6. Will, not going away, gets more intimate with Rosamond, & she more disposed to conquer him.

   7. Will learns the nature of Mr. Casaubon's Will

     .   .   .   .

   11. Will's struggles. Gets an interview with Dorothea. They part.

In *Quarry II*, 31, in a list headed " Remaining Scenes of Part VI," these events are again repeated:

   3. After Will has learned the nature of Mr. Casaubon's codicil.

     .   .   .   .

   6. Will's struggles

   7. Interview between Will & Dorothea. Parting

   8. Will gone away.[11]

It is obvious from the above entries that the details of this portion of the novel were fairly well thought out in advance of the writing but the order had yet to be established. The order of the " Elements of B. VI " entries—Will and Dorothea parting, Will knowing, and Will being flirted with—is more or less reversed in the " *Will . . . Dorothea* " narrative. The " Scenes " add an element not before present, " Will's struggles." In the summary, in the " Scenes," and in the " Remaining Scenes of Part VI " entries, but not in the " Elements of B. VI," this story is broken up by the disclosure by Bulstrode of the relationship between himself and Will. With the addition and expansion of this element, the plan approaches the final stage.

    The integration of the Dorothea and Lydgate elements of the novel through Rosamond's flirtation with Will Ladislaw seems successful, and, in terms of Rosamond's character and Will's unconventional behavior, almost inevitable. Not so the integration of the Garth, Lydgate, and Brooke elements through the Bulstrode-Rigg-Raffles plot. We are ready not to disbelieve the coincidence of Mr. Bulstrode's old associate, Raffles, turning up as Joshua Rigg's stepfather. But to have Will Ladislaw, Casaubon's second cousin, the grandson of Bulstrode's first wife and the rightful heir, whom Raffles has helped Bulstrode keep from his inheritance, and to have them all in this same provincial town miles from where their former association found them, is perhaps too much even for the most indulgent reader to tolerate.

    This set of complicated and coincidental circumstances is revealed in the novel only very slowly and indirectly, but in the notebook six pages of summary—*Quarry II*, 17-22, headed " Sketch I "–" Sketch VI "—are

---

[11] Earlier on this page of the notebook, under " *How to End the Parts,*" there is this entry: " Part VI ends with the Farebrothers telling Dorothea of Will's sudden departure." This is not the case in the novel.

devoted to clarifying the situation. These are the first pages in the notebook written in paragraph form which deal with fictional events. However, they never appear in anything like their notebook form in *Middlemarch*, George Eliot apparently having used the sketches to provide herself with a simplified version of the situation so that she might keep the complicated details straight in her own mind while presenting them piecemeal in the novel.

It is difficult to say just when and how this triple coincidence came about. It certainly was not part of George Eliot's original conception of either " Middlemarch " or " Miss Brooke," since some of the characters involved come from each of the two story elements. Yet now, in *Middlemarch*, it seems prepared for almost from the beginning. In chapter 9, almost certainly written as part of " Miss Brooke," Dorothea comments on the miniature of Will's grandmother that she finds at Lowick Manor. The mystery of her " unfortunate marriage," mentioned by Mr. Casaubon, promises the reader that more is to come from that direction (1: 111-12). It is impossible to believe that at this point the relationship between Ladislaw in " Miss Brooke " and Bulstrode and Raffles in " Middlemarch " was foreseen, but impossible also to ascertain just what use was to have been made of this mystery of Will Ladislaw's origin, if any. On the other hand, the Bulstrode-Raffles relationship also now seems predicated on Will's parentage, though here it is possible to visualize the situation without Will: Raffles' hold on Bulstrode would have been strong, if not as strong as at present, had he merely known of the banker's association with stolen merchandise, the source of Bulstrode's fortune. The best we can do is conjecture that there was to have been some plot development involving Will's antecedents in " Miss Brooke " and that Raffles was to have had a hold on Bulstrode in " Middlemarch." That the two rather melodramatic plot complications had to be wound into a triply coincidental and melodramatic plot is unfortunate.

Despite George Eliot's preparation of the background in these notebook sketches, and despite the incidents throughout the novel which in some ways prepare the reader for the outcome of this plot development, it is not successful. Rigg and Raffles are the least successful characters in the novel by almost common consent. They are incompletely visualized, incompletely presented. The coincidences are too many. Even with a summary in her notebook George Eliot did not seem capable of realizing the characters and situation, e. g., twice (3: 285 and 367) Will is referred to as the grandson of a " *Jew* pawnbroker " (italics mine), the second time in particular with the author's apparent agreement that the description is accurate even if the attitude behind the remark is to be deplored. But Dunkirk was a member of the same dissenting church to which

Bulstrode belonged, and it was through church activities that the relationship between the two began; nowhere is there any indication that Dunkirk was or ever had been a Jew or that any other relative of Will's could be considered the pawnbroker referred to. This relatively unimportant slip shows, it seems, how weak George Eliot's grasp of the complicated details of this part of the novel was, a weakness also revealed by her needing a long summary of the situation in the notebook. In addition, this mistake may reveal traces of an earlier intention: it may be that in "Miss Brooke" the mystery of Will's birth had to do with his Jewishness. If so, this is an interesting foreshadowing of the situation in the novel George Eliot was to write next, *Daniel Deronda*.[12]

The background sketches for this plot situation start to take fictional form in *Quarry II*, 23, the fourth item in the unheaded list being, "Ladislaw's birth known," following "Scene of Fred Vincy's choice, after Mar. 31" and preceding "Mr. Farebrother's appointment to the living." The Ladislaw element is absent from the list of "Elements" on page 24 and from the list of "Elements of B. VI" on page 26, but in the "*Will . . . Dorothea*" narrative summary on page 27 Will is described as learning "about his mother's family from Bulstrode." Raffles' appearances, meanwhile, are summarized on page 28:

Bulstrode & Raffles

Bulstrode buys Featherstone's land; Rigg having an ideal elsewhere. Raffles, not knowing where to find Bulstrode, his letter being dated from "The Shrubs" & containing no clue, comes again after Rigg, & finds Bulstrode riding about Stone Court. Rigg's ideal is a money-changing business.

Raffles comes again, recognizes Will & tells Bulstrode, who gets Raffles away by payment, & then under conscientious relenting offers amends to Will.

Raffles comes back the third time.

Bulstrode's desire to buy Stone Court and Rigg's willingness to sell appear as early as the end of chapter 40 and in chapter 41, in Book 4, at the time of Raffles' first appearance in the neighborhood, but at that time the reason for Rigg's willingness to sell is not made clear. Rigg's motivation, his "ideal," is presented for the first time in the last chapter of Book 5, chapter 53; it is in this chapter too that we learn that Bulstrode has already purchased Stone Court, and it is here that Raffles returns "& finds Bulstrode riding about Stone Court." The second paragraph of the summary, however, does not appear in *Middlemarch* until late in Book 6, chapter 60, in which Raffles recognizes Will at the auction, the actual setting having been added since the writing of the summary. In chapter 61 Bulstrode tells Will and offers him money to make partial amends, but is refused.

[12] See my article, "The Forgotten Past of Will Ladislaw," in *Nineteenth-Century Fiction*, 13 (1958), 159-63.

The summary in the notebook is followed by the list of " Scenes " on page 29 in which the information from paragraph two of the summary contained in items 8, 9, and 10:

8 Raffles comes back & recognizes Will
9 Raffles tells Bulstrode who Will is.
10 Bulstrode paying Raffles to go away, makes offers to Will, constrained by fear & conscience.

To this last item George Eliot added a footnote, apparently seeing a further relationship between this plot line and that of Lydgate and Dorothea: " Bulstrode expecting to be cramped for money induces Dorothea to do more for the Hospital." The details from the list of " Scenes," without the footnote, appear a third time in the list of " Remaining Scenes of Part VI ":

4 Raffles returns & recognizes Will & tells Bulstrode.
5 Scene between Bulstrode & Will

Thus this portion of Book 6 does not undergo much change in the notebook planning stage after it is first established. The actual setting of Raffles' recognition of Will—the auction—was never made clear, perhaps was not thought of, during the prewriting stages of the planning.

Quarry plans for Book 6 are more extensive than they are for any previous part of *Middlemarch*. In these plans, therefore, for the first time something like a method in the development of the novel is evident. In the earliest stages of planning the various strands of the novel were relatively separate, viz., " Sketches," pp. 17-22. Then, lists were made of the major situations and happenings, though neither their order nor the number per part was yet settled, viz., " Elements," p. 24. These situations and happenings were then grouped to approximate one part, the order still not too clear, viz., " Elements of B. VI," p. 26. Because the order and relationship were not clear, the strands were still separate, viz., " *Will Ladislaw & Dorothea*," p. 27, and " Bulstrode & Raffles," p. 28. These major events began to take on the form of dramatic scenes, of chapters, and the strands began, now that some sort of order had been established, to be related one to the other, viz., " Scenes," pp. 29-30. With the establishment of the major situations and happenings in scenes and chapters, and with the relationships between the various strands of the novel shaping up, the writing of the part apparently began, new scenes and relationships suggested themselves, and the part as a unit again became a consideration, viz., " *How to End the Parts* " and " Remaining Scenes of Part VI," p. 31. Finally, once the part was completed, the chapters were listed one by one and the total number of manuscript pages in the part was recorded, viz., p. 13. There was still time to change the point at which the part ends, e. g., Book 4 ends now with chapter 42, not, as the pagination of the manuscript reveals was originally intended, with chapter 41—or even to change the order of the chapters, e. g., chapters 57 and 58 have been transposed since the chapter listing on page 13 was drawn up.

This process, then, is about what one would expect, except for the considerable and continuous fluidity of the novel in the hands of the author: the major events were more or less clear in the author's mind, though not, perhaps, too far in advance—e. g., Rosamond's miscarrying had not been foreseen at the time the list of " Private dates " on page 4 was made—but the exact sequence of events was not foreseen, nor were the countless little interrelationships which go to make up the unity of *Middlemarch*. Any number of novelists would have been capable of conceiving even the most advanced and detailed plans of the notebook; only George Eliot from these notes could have written *Middlemarch*.

5.

The benefits of George Eliot's stay at Redhill lasted at least until she completed Book 7. On August 4, in a letter to John Blackwood, she spoke of a " bilious attack " which kept her from work on the last part of *Middlemarch*, so that even then Book 7 must have been completed, though Lewes, mailing it on August 9, spoke of unfortunate delay. Book 6 had been mailed only five weeks before, so the pace was now swift enough to keep George Eliot well ahead of publication dates. Book 5 had just been published, Book 6 was not due for another two months, the speed-up to monthly publication not being scheduled until the November appearance of Book 7.

Meanwhile, the first parts of *Middlemarch* had been a critical success, and, for a publishing experiment, sales had been gratifying if not so great as the optimistic Lewes had anticipated. The big success of the novel was to come later, unexpectedly, in the sale of the cheaper editions.[13]

One of the reasons George Eliot was able to write Book 7 so much more quickly than she had written the preceding parts, perhaps, was that

---

[13] See Blackwood's report, *Letters* 5: 298, which shows sales averages just under 5,000 per part and dropping. Lewes had expected to sell 10,000 copies of each part according to his letter to Blackwood on August 21, 1871. Early in 1874, before the cheap edition (7/6) was published, some 8,500 copies of *Middlemarch* in all editions (parts, 2 gns. and one gn.) had been disposed of (*Letters* 6: 10). In the first six months or so the cheap edition sold well over 10,000 copies; though we have come to expect large sales in cheaper editions, at that time such had not been the case. Blackwood said, " No previous experience could have led us to expect such a rapid and extended sale in the 7/6 form " (*Letters* 6: 114). By the end of 1875, over 14,500 copies of the edition were sold (*Letters* 6: 204); by the end of 1878, almost 31,000 (*Letters* 7: 364).

the plans for the earlier parts had been extensive enough to cover the development of the last parts of the novel. The planning which went into Book 6, especially the sketches, the summaries, and the long list of "Scenes" in *Quarry II*, 29-30, involved not only that part but the two remaining parts of *Middlemarch* as well. The very chapter titles of Book 7, listed in *Quarry II*, 14, recall some of the items from these lists:

63 New Year. Mr. Farebrother & Lydgate
64 Lydgate & Rosamond: house-letting
65 Sir Godwin's letter comes.
66 Lydgate in the Billiard Room: Fred called by Mr. Farebrother
67 Lydgate applies to Bulstrode
68 Bulstrode's late experience, & consequent plans.
69 Caleb Garth informs Bulstrode that Raffles is at Stone Court. Lydgate called in. Goes home & finds the execution in his house.
70 Bulstrode's state of mind about Raffles–& Lydgate.
    Gives Lydgate the cheque for 1000. Struggles.
    Gives the key to the housekeeper. *Death.*
71 Scandal in Middlemarch. Mr. Hawley's outburst against Bulstrode. Dorothea enters.

Of these chapters, the underlying situation of the first two and the chief detail of the third have already been mentioned in the planning of Book 6: in *Quarry II*, 26, in the list of " Elements of B. VI "–" Lydgate gets more embarrassed, & moody in consequence/ Rosamond makes him angry by writing his uncle "—and in the list of " Scenes," page 29— " 5 Lydgate embarrassed more & more, is moody. Rosamond, discontented, writes to Sir Godwin. Sir Godwin replies to Lydgate. His anger with R." The general situation of the last three chapters also is to be found in the plans which otherwise chiefly apply to Book 6. The last three " Elements " on page 24 are:

10 Lydgate attends Raffles' deathbed
11 Accepts money from Bulstrode
12 Scandal blighting him & Bulstrode

The last three " Scenes " on page 30 are:

20 Raffles comes back. Terror of Bulstrode. Disclosures.
21 Raffles' death. Bulstrode gives Lydgate £1000.
22 Scandal in Middlemarch. Blight on Lydgate & Bulstrode . . .

Finally, under "*How to End the Parts*," page 31, Book 7 " Ends with Lydgate's bribe." [14] And, it will be noted, although the general course of the first three and of the last three chapters of Book 7 was given in that portion of *Quarry II* devoted primarily to the planning of Book 6,

[14] Miss Kitchel (p. 38) notes that above this entry George Eliot had written " outpouring," and, presumably, added " to Dorothea." In the " Part VII " list (*Quarry II*, 34) " Outpouring to Dorothea " is last and George Eliot later enclosed it in square brackets and marked it " Part VIII," where it now appears.

i. e., from the first sketch of Bulstrode's history on page 17 to " Remaining Scenes of Part VI " on page 31, which was the last entry having anything to do with this part, there were no concrete details or scenes for these six chapters or for the middle three chapters in Book 7.

The plans for the first three chapters of Book 7 reveal little of the stages of development. On page 34, in the list headed " Part VII," they are called simply " Lydgate's affairs," and on page 38, as part of the " *Course of Part VII*," they are already in their final form:

1   Mr. Farebrother makes advances to Lydgate—refused.
2   Lydgate trying to get rid of his house: Rosd. thwarts him
3   Difficulties increase   Sir Godwin's letter comes

This page is the last in the notebook devoted to planning Book 7; the twelve items listed there make up the nine chapters of the part and appear in the same order. The intrigue involving Sir Godwin's letter had been prepared for in the plans for Book 6, as we have seen, but Farebrother's offer and the house-letting episode are new to the debt situation. It is even possible that they were already written into the novel when this note was made.

The middle three chapters went through more stages. In the list headed " Part VII," two items and part of a third found their way into these chapters: item 2, " Fred & Mary," apparently referred to that part of chapter 66 in which Farebrother warns Fred that he may lose Mary if he is not careful; " 3   Bulstrode's terrors & wish to get rid of the hospital," was footnoted by George Eliot in the notebook, " Action of Caleb Garth," and forms chapter 68, the footnote apparently referring to the beginning of chapter 69; " 4   Lydgate sounds him. He is deaf . . ." is the first mention of Lydgate's attempt to borrow money from Bulstrode, which appears in chapter 67. As is usual with these early plans, their order is not that of the final version.

The summary of these scenes and events which follows this first list, *Quarry II*, 35, is much more detailed but leaves out Lydgate's seeking to borrow from Bulstrode:

Lydgate goes to the Billiard room at G. D.
   (letter comes from Sir Godwin)
Fred Vincy is in the Billiard room
Mr. Farebrother sends up for him
Walks with Fred to St. Botolph's Parsonage & admonishes him that if he is not to lose Mary he must be careful.
Raffles having again been to Middlemarch—(seen by Lydgate in the billiard room) Bulstrode is meditating removal from Middlemarch going somewhere where he will have a less marked position & suffer less from the visits of Raffles. Is engaged in transferring his bank, & arranging the rest of his property for management without his personal presence. Is seeing Caleb Garth on the subject.

This is a rather full statement of the details and relationships to be found in chapters 66-68, bringing together the Lydgate and Fred-Mary stories via the billiard room scene and the Bulstrode-Raffles (-Lydgate) and Garth-Fred-Mary stories via the banker's plans to flee Middlemarch. Besides the omission of Lydgate's applying to the banker for a loan, there are two differences between this summary and the final text of the novel: the letter has arrived from Sir Godwin before the billiard room scene, and Raffles has visited Bulstrode again at Christmas and is not seen by Lydgate in the billiard room—the parentheses around these two items in the notebook George Eliot probably put there when she changed her plans.

The penultimate " *Course of Part VII* " more or less repeats the details of this summary and brings it into line with the final version by omitting the two parenthetical items and adding Lydgate's application to Bulstrode for a loan:

4 Lydgate goes to the billiard room. Fred Vincy is there:
   Mr. Farebrother comes to fetch him.
5 Fred Vincy & he walk together
6 Lydgate begins to think of applying to Bulstrode.
   Bulstrode's efforts to free himself & wish to quit Middlemarch—business with Caleb Garth.
7 Lydgate sounds Bulstrode

The three middle chapters of Book 7 were almost in their final form, but still a little had to be done. Lydgate's " sounding " of Bulstrode was joined to his thinking " of applying to Bulstrode " to form chapter 67, thus preceding Bulstrode's preparations for departure and making the " business with Caleb Garth " serve as a transition to chapter 69, in which Caleb picks up the dying Raffles.

The pattern of development of these chapters is much the same as that which was apparent in the building up of Book 6. The rather vague topics—" Lydgate's affairs," " Fred & Mary," " Bulstrode's terrors & wish to get rid of the hospital. Action of Caleb Garth," and " Lydgate sounds him. He is deaf "—here found on page 34, were on the next page in the notebook clothed in flesh, written as scenes with underlying relationships. Then George Eliot changed some of the events, added some unforeseen details (e. g., Raffles' Christmas visit) , and, finally, changed the order of events to make the relationships of and transitions from one portion of the plot to the other smooth and inevitable.

The last three chapters of Book 7 contain the most important series of events in this part, and, perhaps, in the entire last portion of the novel: Raffles' death, Lydgate's " bribe," and the consequent scandal. These events, enumerated as early as the list of " Elements " on page 24 and again in the list of " Scenes " on page 30, were planned, at least in part, almost page by page in *Quarry II*, 33, even before the planning of the billiard room scene, etc. of the middle three chapters:

Mr. Farebrother comes to Lydgate to see if anything can be done for him. Finds him in high spirits, released from trouble. Hears him speak of Raffles' illness.

α   Bambridge tells what he has heard
β   Raffles identified as just buried
γ   Diffusion of the scandal among the Middlemarchers in connexion with Lydgate's release from debt
δ   Scandal spreads to Freshitt & Lowick
ε   Mr. Hawley explodes at Vestry meeting
ζ   Lydgate's misery. Rosamond's repulsion
η   Mrs. Bulstrode

All of these events, of course, are subsequent to Raffles' death. Farebrother's visit to Lydgate takes place immediately after Raffles dies, indeed in the very chapter (chap. 70; 3: 275-78) , but in that scene in the novel Lydgate does not speak of Raffles—instead Hawley later tells Farebrother of the scandal involving Bulstrode (chap. 71; 3: 284-85) , and Mr. Farebrother himself makes the connection between Raffles' death and Lydgate's having borrowed money from Bulstrode, though he tries to keep Hawley from making the same connection. Chapter 71 opens with Bambridge in front of the Green Dragon (3: 279-81) . The items in the list follow immediately in the novel:

α   3: 281
β   3: 282
γ   3: 286-93, from 288 on being the gossip scene at Dollop's
δ   3: 293, Tipton and Lowick not Freshitt and Lowick specified
ε   3: 294-301, but Hawley explodes at a meeting " on the sanitary question " concerning cholera not at a " Vestry meeting."

The last two items on the list, *zeta* and *eta*, however, appear in later chapters.

Plans for the events surrounding Raffles' death are the most detailed thus far in the notebook. Plans for chapters 66 and 68, ending with Bulstrode's preparations for leaving Middlemarch, and the even more detailed plans for part of chapter 70 and for chapter 71, the scandal following Raffles' death, have already been quoted. Following the latter (*Quarry II*, 35-36) are equally specific plans, chiefly for the intervening chapters 69, 70, and, in part, 71, the events leading directly up to the death of Raffles (though the plans carry the story beyond that point) :

Hence Caleb is going to Stone Court on business.
  Overtakes Raffles who is ill
takes him up in his gig. Raffles tells Caleb everything about Bulstrode
(Raffles has also told Bambridge)

(36)

That Raffles should tell the whole story of Bulstrode to Caleb Garth; that Caleb should remain silent on the subject even to his wife.

That Raffles should tell Bulstrode how Caleb knew all—but no one else than Caleb.

That Bulstrode sounds Caleb, who tells him his reasons for never disclosing

Caleb calls on Bulstrode tells him that Raffles is at Stone Court & in need of a doctor.

Also declines to act further for Bulstrode.

Bulstrode calls in Lydgate.

Gives orders to the woman who sits up with Raffles, to administer opium & alcohol

Gives Lydgate the thousand pounds

Mr. Farebrother, not knowing comes with help.

Lydgate's anguish. Rosamond's repulsion

Scene of outburst at a Vestry meeting in which Mr. Hawley tells Bulstrode that he is known.

Lydgate pours out to Dorothea about his misery, & she comforts him.[15]

The list on page 36 appears to be a new beginning rather than a continuation of page 35, since it repeats the last three sentences of page 35, except for the parenthetical remark, and starts out with a new " that " construction. The first five items on page 36 present a detailed account of what was to be chapter 69, but without any mention of Lydgate's finding " the execution in his house." Even the details which did find their way from this list into chapter 69 did so in a somewhat different form: the events on pages 35-36 were recounted chronologically and omnisciently, whereas in the novel these events are presented more or less from Bulstrode's point of view, and thus we learn of them as he does, from Caleb Garth upon his arrival at the bank after he has picked up Raffles and left him at Stone Court. This presentation of the material enabled George Eliot to condense it into a single Bulstrode-Caleb scene which itself necessitated certain modifications of or additions to the details as listed in the notebook: " Bulstrode calls in Lydgate " in the novel by asking Garth to fetch him, then changing his mind and sending a servant (3: 247) ; Bulstrode learns that Raffles has told Garth all, not from Raffles as planned but from Garth (3: 248) , Raffles at first denying that he has told anyone (3: 253) , an added twist which makes his

---

[15] George Eliot enclosed this last sentence and " Lydgate's anguish. Rosamond's repulsion " in square brackets and marked them " VIII." The last two unmarked items in this list make up the end of chapter 70 and chapter 71, the same chapters which received such detailed treatment on page 33, *Quarry II*, which intervenes between two pages devoted to Will and Dorothea and must have been left blank and filled in later, probably after George Eliot had written *Quarry II*, 34-36—the last two Book 7 items on page 36 are detailed on this page; the chapters (end of 70 and 71) dealt with on this page are later than those (69 and beginning of 70) dealt with on pages 35-36.

having told Bambridge the more believable. With just these minor changes, that which was two scenes in the notebook could become one scene in the novel.

The sixth item on page 36—" [Bulstrode] gives orders to the woman who sits up with Raffles, to administer opium & alcohol "—was also significantly changed, and improved, by the time it appeared in chapter 70: Bulstrode scrupulously orders Mrs. Abel to give only the dosage of opium prescribed by Lydgate and no alcohol at all, but he neglects to tell her when to stop administering opium; he is about to go to her to impart this information, hesitates, quibbles with himself about the wisdom of Lydgate's advice, and goes to his bedroom, where Mrs. Abel almost immediately knocks and asks for brandy to give the suffering Raffles; Bulstrode struggles with himself as the housekeeper continues to advise brandy, and he thrusts the key to the wine-cooler through the door (3: 268-71). The effect of this change is greatly to deepen and " realize " the portrait of Bulstrode: he now does not perpetrate evil but simply yields to an overwhelming temptation which he can disguise as the will of God. Even Bulstrode, living in his two distinct and unrelated worlds of prayer and profit, would have difficulty in reconciling deliberate disobedience of Lydgate for purposes of murder with his conscience. Like Rosamond's miscarriage, this new version of the events of the novel evidently occurred to the author between the time she made the notebook plans and the time she wrote the pertinent portion of the novel, perhaps in the very act of writing itself. This sudden occurrence of new insights happens to all writers and is sometimes referred to as the characters' carrying away the author, acting on their own, performing deeds and uttering dialogue that the author was unconscious of preparing or even thinking of in advance. This interaction of the writer and his medium, however, does not mean that at these moments he is writing *unconsciously*, that his critical faculties are necessarily asleep or his reason suspended. What it does mean is simply that the very act of writing, the very necessity of embodying the abstract or undetailed outline in the concrete and detailed work of art is the essential, all-important act, which no amount of planning or outlining of intentions can completely explain or replace. The plans and outlines are only the author's " ideas "; the novel is his work of art. Any number of writers could have written George Eliot's notebooks; only she could have written *Middlemarch*.

That same process of change and enrichment is evident in the evolution of the seventh item—" Gives Lydgate the thousand pounds "—into the episode in the novel. The bare notebook item does not prepare us for the subtle reasoning of the banker and his motivation. For in the novel, the loan is granted *before* the " murder," in order to gain Lydgate's friendship and obligation in case Raffles should make embarrassing revelations in his presence (3: 263-64), though in the notebook list the loan is granted only *after* the "murder." The notion of murder had not yet consciously occurred to Bulstrode, though he of course saw the advantage to himself of Raffles' death and could not but wish for that death— "Thy will be done," but how convenient it would be if Thy will coincided with my will, or, at least, with my best interests—and the notion of Raffles' death immediately associated in the banker's mind with Lydgate's treatment (3: 262-63), and was immediately followed by Bulstrode's decision to loan the doctor the thousand pounds. Similarly, Lydgate, in accepting the loan before Raffles died could in no way associate the money with the death; the loan became a very subtle bribe only in that Lydgate, after Raffles' death, though puzzled by the fact of the death which he did not expect, was disposed not to ask the banker questions because of his obligations to him:

he was conscious that Bulstrode had been a benefactor to him. But he was uneasy about this case. He had not expected it to tenminate [*sic*] as it had done. Yet he hardly knew how to put a question on the subject to Bulstrode without appearing to insult him; and if he examined the housekeeper—why, the man was dead. There seemed to be no use in implying that somebody's ignorance or imprudence had killed him. And after all, he himself might be wrong (3: 274).

The intermediate stage between the plans on pp. 35-36 in the notebook and the final forms of chapters 69 and 70 is evident in the "*Course of Part VII*" in *Quarry II*, 38, the last step in the planning before the chapters were written:

8 Caleb Garth picks up Raffles. Takes him to Stone Court. Raffles tells him the secrets
9 Caleb calls on Bulstrode, who tells him Raffles is there & declines further transactions. Bulstrode suspects the reasons. Caleb reassures him as to secrecy. Execution in Lydgate's house.
10 Bulstrode having called in Lydgate, neglects his orders, & causes Raffles to take alcohol etc.
11 Bulstrode calls on Lydgate & gives him £1000 or £500 (?)

Certain important changes had already been made: it is Garth and not Raffles who reveals that he is now party to the secrets about Bulstrode's past by refusing to work for the banker any longer; the execution in Lydgate's house had by now been added, and, most important, Bulstrode no longer "gives orders" that result in Raffles' death, but "neglects" Lydgate's orders and thereby "causes Raffles to take alcohol." Equally important changes had not yet been made in this last planning stage and had to await the actual writing of the chapters: Caleb Garth still picks up Raffles and learns the secrets prior to and in a separate scene from that in which Bulstrode learns of this action—though it may be argued that this list accurately states the incidents in the order in which they occur though it differs from the order in which the incidents are made apparent in the novel—and, most important, the " bribe " still follows the death of Raffles (here necessitating a separate scene in which Bulstrode calls on Lydgate, whereas in the novel the loan takes place at Stone Court where Lydgate had been called to attend Raffles). That Bulstrode " neglects " Lydgate's orders is closer to the final version than his giving contradicting orders himself, but it still does not approach the inner conflict which racks Bulstrode in the novel after he has forgotten to tell the housekeeper when to stop administering opium and the even greater conflict when she appears at his door asking permission to give Raffles brandy; these developments also must await the writing stage itself.

Book 7, then, follows the pattern of development from notebook to novel first clearly seen in the plans for Book 6. The separate " Miss Brooke " and " Middlemarch " stories no longer existed and there was no attempt to interrelate them any more closely than the plot demanded. The main situations and incidents—in this case Lydgate's increasing difficulties, his being extricated from these difficulties by a loan from Bulstrode which, with Raffles dead, appears to have been a bribe, and the scandal about Bulstrode's pre-Middlemarch activities which bursts upon that provincial town and arouses grave suspicions about the death of Raffles and the roles of both the banker and the doctor—had been in George Eliot's mind and notebook before she considered Book 7 as a part, i. e., in the list of " Elements " in *Quarry II*, 24. Even before she completed Book 6 these events began to take the shape of " Scenes " (*Quarry II*, 30). Then she very briefly sketched out the main events which were to form the part (" Part VII," p. 34). In the plans for Book 7 there was an additional and more detailed stage of planning for each of the chapters: even after she considered the scenes a part (" Part VII " list on p. 34), she planned the settings and particular scenes themselves in detail (pp. 33 and 35-36). Once again George Eliot considered the material as a part: " Conclusion of Part VII," p. 37, and " *Course of Part VII*," p. 38. All the while she tightened the relationships among incidents as they became chapters and changed significant and insignificant but telling aspects of the incidents and their sequence. Finally, between the last of the prewriting plans, " *Course of Part VII*," and the postwriting list of chapters within the part on page 14, i. e., apparently in the process of writing itself, she perceived other important events, motives, and sequences, unforeseen and unplanned for, so that the finished chapters do not resemble even the latest and most detailed of the plans in the notebook in some very important respects.

6.

One important change in plans involving Book 7 has not been discussed, for it involves Book 8 as well and will be considered now as one aspect of the development of the last part of *Middlemarch*.

Once into the last part of *Middlemarch*, George Eliot was anxious to be quit of it, and there are evident signs of haste as she approached the end of the novel. On August 22, just two weeks after he had mailed Book 7, Lewes wrote William Blackwood that he hoped the return to the Priory from Redhill would " do Mrs. Lewes some good although I give up all hope of any permanent good until the book is finally out of hand and she can take a holiday." He sent the manuscript to the publisher piecemeal: he mailed the first ninety manuscript pages, through chapter 80, on September 2 and requested proof in a week; he mailed thirty more pages exactly a week later and requested proof by Thursday, September 12; he mailed another eighteen pages two days later, but the departure for Hamburg had been delayed slightly—"if we get a proof on Monday it will be time enough, as we go to a friend's near Cambridge for Saturday and Sunday and return on Monday to start for Hamburg "; he mailed the final two chapters on Friday the thirteenth.[16] *Middlemarch*, except for the " Finale," which was sent October 2, was now complete.

The final list of chapters of that part in the notebook (p. 15) reflects this haste—there was really no longer any purpose in keeping such a list, which was, in effect, a progress report and record. After the first three chapter titles, George Eliot for the most part simply jotted down the names of the chief characters involved in the chapter. For the last chapter, 86, there is only a number, no title or name at all:

72 Dorothea wants to help Lydgate—.
73 Lydgate's first anguish
74 Mrs. Bulstrode learns her sorrow
75 Rosamond & Lydgate
76 Lydgate & Dorothea
77 Dorothea, Rosamond & Will Ladislaw
78 Will & Rosamond
79 afterwards Will & Lydgate
80 Dorothea in her anguish
81 Dorothea & Rosamond
82 Will Ladislaw
83 Will & Dorothea
84 Mr. Brooke carries news
85 Mr. & Mrs. Bulstrode
86

The chief function of this last part of *Middlemarch* is to tie up all

---

[16] See *Letters* 7: 390, " Addenda and Corrigenda."

the loose ends of plot: to particularize the fates of Lydgate and Bulstrode, to get Fred and Mary married and settled at Stone Court, and at last to get Will and Dorothea married. Only the last of these required any fresh incidents, the rest coming as the direct or indirect result of the Bulstrode scandal. It was George Eliot's effort to get Will and Dorothea together which resulted in the change affecting Book 7 as well as Book 8.

That Will and Dorothea were to get married, much to the chagrin of some readers, had been decided upon from the time the very earliest plans for *Middlemarch* were entered in the notebook: " Dorothea's second marriage " appears in the list of " Private dates " on *Quarry II*, 4. What had since been changed was the timing of that marriage, though just when the change was made is uncertain. In the list on page 4, the marriage is dated " 1832 Jan. or Feb.," and the death of Raffles is dated " Aug. 1832." The sequence of these events is reversed in the list of " Motives (in general) " on page 11, for in this list the " Blight on Bulstrode & Lydgate " which follows Raffles' death is followed by three items—" Rosamond's flirtation with Ladislaw/ Dorothea after severe struggles goes to Rosamond/ Action of Caleb Garth & Mr. Farebrother "— the first two of which very closely resemble the actual events in the middle chapters of Book 8 and rather clearly indicate that Will and Dorothea, as in the novel, were not to have been married at the time the scandal about Lydgate and Bulstrode broke. It seems likely, however, that George Eliot added these three items on page 11 long after she wrote the rest of the list, and indeed after she wrote most of the rest of the notebook, for plans much later in the notebook follow the sequence of events described in the earlier list, " Private dates," not the sequence on page 11 and in the novel. Among the list of " Elements " on page 24, for example, item 9 is the " Second marriage of Dorothea " and is followed by: " 10   Lydgate attends Raffles' deathbed/ 11   Accepts money from Bulstrode/ 12   Scandal blighting him & Bulstrode." Even later than the list of " Elements " on page 24, the Will-Dorothea plot was treated before the Bulstrode-Raffles-Lydgate plot. Preceding the " Bulstrode & Raffles " summary on page 28 is the summary headed " *Will Ladislaw & Dorothea* " on page 27, which earlier in this chapter has been quoted through its description of the second meeting and parting of Will and Dorothea; it continues from that point:

She finds him with Mrs. Lydgate. Scene between her & Will—anger, jealousy, reproach, ending in Dorothea's passionate avowal, & declaration that she will never marry him. Will reproaches Rosamond with having ruined his happiness. Rosamond alarmed lest Dorothea should tell Lydgate. Dorothea goes to R. having conquered her jealousy by pity, & hears that Will has been true to her.

There is no mention in this summary of the marriage of Will and Doro-

thea, but in the list of "Scenes" on pages 29-30 this marriage is introduced immediately after the events of the summary:

12 Will vacillating goes to Rosamond
13 Dorothea discovers them in emotion—together
14 Scene of anger & jealousy between Will & Dorothea, ending in her avowal
    of love & resolve not to marry him
15 Will goes to Rosamond & reproaches her with having ruined his happiness.
16 Dorothea, wrought on by compassion, goes to Rosamond, & so moves
    her that R. tells D. how Will has been true.
17 Meeting & final reconciliation of Will & Dorothea.
18 Dorothea declares to Sir James her intention to marry Will

Here all of these items immediately follow the parting scene between
Will and Dorothea which ends Book 6. This sequence would have done
away with the present necessity in the novel for Will to go away from
Middlemarch and to return, but this sequence was not adhered to. The
nineteenth item—"Lydgate in difficulties has half made up his mind to
ask Dorothea for aid, & learns that she is going to marry Will"—was in
this earlier plan to have served as a transition between the Will-Dorothea
story and Raffles' death, the "bribe," and the scandal which were to have
followed. The plan of first treating the Will-Dorothea plot and then
the Lydgate-Bulstrode-Raffles plot apparently continued in force to the
very last stage of the planning and probably even through the writing
of Book 6, for immediately after the last entry in the notebook having
to do with that part, "Remaining Scenes of Part VI" on page 31, there
is a summary of the events in the Will-Dorothea plot from the time of
their second parting to their final reconciliation:

Sketch 2 [17]

Will declares his indifference as to what becomes of him & what career he shall
pursue since the only woman he loves is debarred from him by honour. Departs.
Mrs. Cadwallader lets drop some phrase indicating some flirtation between Mrs.
Lydgate & Will, (in Dorothea's hearing).
Scene between Lydgate & Dorothea in which he exposes his whole life. Estrangement between him & Rosamond—her indifference to everything but Ladislaw
& his singing etc. Dorothea writes to him lending the sum: takes it herself to
his house that it may fall into no other hands: also wishing to speak to Rosamond
in the way of counsel—
   Meanwhile Will has returned impatient to hear something about Dorothea.
   Calls on Lydgate. Rosamond who has been pining for him, overjoyed at his
presence—thinks it is for her & pours out her feeling
   Means to go to Utopia

(34)

Dorothea enters. Their confusion. Will hurriedly departs. Rosamond shivering.

---

[17] Apparently so called because George Eliot considered " *Will Ladislaw & Dorothea* "
on page 27 to be "Sketch 1" of this plot line.

Dorothea repressing her anguish, carries out her intended admonition, & quits Rosamond.

Scene between Will & Dorothea

It was evidently at this point in the notebook that George Eliot decided to treat the Raffles incident first. She drew a line across page 34 and made up the list headed " Part VII " which includes Raffles' death and the scandal but not the final reconciliation between Will and Dorothea. From that point on she treated Book 7 as that part having to do with Raffles, etc., and Book 8 as that part having to do chiefly with Will and Dorothea. (It was probably about this time that she added to the list of " Motives (in general) " on page 11.)

Even a cursory comparison between the plans for the last events in the Will-Dorothea plot and the chapters in *Middlemarch* presenting those events reveals that more has been changed than the position of these events relative to Raffles' death and its consequence. Even during the planning stage significant changes had taken place. The main outlines of the early plans in the " *Will Ladislaw & Dorothea* " summary are correct: Dorothea does find Will with Rosamond; Will does reproach Rosamond; Dorothea does come back to Rosamond and learns from her that Will " has been true to her." But there is no suggestion in this summary that between Will and Dorothea's second parting scene Will has left Middlemarch and has only now, when Dorothea finds him with Rosamond, returned. Nor is there any explanation in the summary of why Dorothea is going to Lydgate's or in what state she finds Will and Mrs. Lydgate together. The summary projects a scene of " anger, jealousy, reproach, ending in Dorothea's passionate avowal, & declaration that she will never marry him," but in chapter 77, Dorothea said nothing of the sort; she simply excused herself and " laid down the letter on the small table which had checked her retreat, and then including Rosamond and Will in one distant glance and bow, she went quickly out of the room . . ." (3: 371-72). Finally, in the novel there is more motivation for Dorothea's return to Lydgate's than her simply having " conquered her jealousy by pity ": she has to convince Mrs. Lydgate that her husband has been unjustly slandered by the gossip in Middlemarch.

The next plans, the " Scenes " on pages 29-30, differ from the events in the novel in much the same way, but it is clear that Dorothea finds Will and Rosamond " in emotion—together." This list also carries the action beyond that of the summary, to the " Meeting & final reconcilia- tion of Will & Dorothea," and beyond even that, to the spreading of the news of their intention to marry. In doing so, another item which was to be changed in the novel appears: " Dorothea declares to Sir James her intention to marry Will." This news in chapter 84 is carried by Mr. Brooke.

"Sketch 2" adds a great deal to the summary and "Scenes" in the way of preparation, motivation, and circumstance. The sketch begins with two aspects of chapter 62, the last chapter in Book 6—the ambiguity of Will's remarks about his love (do they apply to Dorothea or to Rosamond?) in his farewell to Dorothea, and Mrs. Cadwallader's gossip in Dorothea's presence concerning Will and Mrs. Lydgate—though in that chapter the order is reversed, Mrs. Cadwallader's gossip preparing Dorothea to see an ambiguous twist to Will's farewell speech, which he thinks overly direct. Though the notebook does not suggest it, in the novel Mrs. Cadwallader's remarks are deliberately made in Dorothea's hearing at the request of Sir James. These elements in the last chapter of Book 6 skillfully prepare for Dorothea's hasty jealousy in chapter 77 of Book 8, and they are all the more effective because of the delay of the events until Book 8, giving the preparation, as it were, time to become part of the reader's understanding of the situation. For example, Mrs. Cadwallader's gossip presented in chapter 62 is referred to in chapter 77, right before Dorothea visits Mrs. Lydgate (3: 365), and just as it is in the back of Dorothea's mind when she visits the Lydgates, so it is in the back of the reader's mind as part of the circumstances of the novel. The third item of the sketch, having to do with the Lydgate-Dorothea scene which now forms chapter 76, was only partially carried out as here planned. Lydgate does suggest an "estrangement between him & Rosamond," but it is much less direct and more gentlemanly than the notebook's suggestion that he accuse her of "indifference to everything but Ladislaw & his singing etc." The shadow of Ladislaw on the Lydgates' hearth was left to Dorothea to cast, especially since at the time of this conversation Will has not yet returned to Middlemarch and is thus not part of Lydgate's vision of his home and its present difficulties—he has more important things to worry about than Rosamond's attitude toward Will Ladislaw. The first items of this sketch, containing as they do elements of the last chapter of Book 6 and continuing the Will-Dorothea plot from that point, suggest that the sketch was written while it was still George Eliot's purpose to include the Will-Dorothea story in Book 7, but the beginning of the fourth item of the sketch—"Dorothea writes to him [Lydgate] lending the sum"—presents a difficulty in this interpretation: if Dorothea's loan preceded Lydgate's treatment of Raffles, why was Bulstrode's loan necessary? Is it possible that with this item the present sequence of events—Raffles first, Dorothea-Will second—had begun working itself out? On the other hand, it is possible that the relationship between Dorothea's loan and Bulstrode's had not been determined as yet. So, too, the exact meaning of the last part of this item—" [Dorothea] also wishing to speak to Rosamond in the way of counsel "—is ambiguous: does this counsel simply relate to her " carryings on " with Will, or, as in the novel, to her attitude toward the gossip about Lydgate's connection with Raffles' death? The events in the novel follow these notebook suggestions rather closely, and it is likely that it was about the time this sketch was drawn that George Eliot decided to treat the Raffles incidents in Book 7 and the Will-Dorothea story in Book 8. The sketch continues with Will's returning to Middlemarch, " impatient to hear something about Dorothea." This is, by and large, accurate in view of the description of his return in the novel. Lydgate himself suspects " that Dorothea was the real cause of . . . [Will's] present visit to Middlemarch " (3: 383) (so Lydgate could not have been too jealous of his wife's attention to Will and his singing, etc.) , and Will admits as much to himself (3: 410-11) , though he gives a public reason and a private excuse: he must see whether it would be moral to use his hold on Bulstrode to get money for a " settlement on a new plan in the Far West " (3: 411) .[18] The scene between Will and Rosamond is not presented directly, as suggested by the sixth item of the sketch, but indirectly, by the tableau that the reader sees through Dorothea's eyes and by Rosamond's correcting that impression in her later conversation with Dorothea (chap. 81) . Apparently the seventh item—" [Will] means to go to Utopia "—was to have been part of his scene with Rosamond, but in the novel his plans for a new settlement appear only as the alleged cause of his return to Middlemarch at this time. The continuation of the sketch on page 34 indicates that when Dorothea interrupts Will and Rosamond, he leaves, and Dorothea at that point has her interview with Rosamond. In the novel it is Dorothea who leaves and must, after a struggle with herself, force herself to return to complete her " mission of mercy " to Mrs. Lydgate for reasons which have nothing to do with Will. It is difficult, even now, for cynical moderns to accept Dorothea's conquering of her own emotions sufficiently to carry out her selfless mission by returning to Lydgate's; how much more incredible would it have been had George Eliot presented Dorothea carrying out her mission immediately after finding Will alone with Rosamond under rather suspicious circumstances!

The notebook sketch, though neither complete nor in final form, nevertheless established the major portion of what was to be Book 8 of *Middlemarch*. Since it was about the time she wrote the sketch, however,

---

[18] Will's visit was prepared for earlier in the novel by his letter to Lydgate suggesting that such a visit may be necessary and speaking of " his new interest in plans of colonization " (3: 339) .

that George Eliot decided that the Will-Dorothea incidents were to be in the last and not in the seventh part of the novel, she ceased planning these incidents and took up those of the actual Book 7—Raffles' death, etc. But even in later plans for the new Book 7, scenes and situations that were eventually to appear in Book 8 were still included among the details of the earlier part. Twice, for example, once in the list on page 34 headed "Part VII" and again on page 36, the scene in which Lydgate tells Dorothea about his personal affairs (now chapter 76) was included among the plans for Book 7. On both occasions the entry was enclosed in square brackets and marked "VIII," as it later became clear to the author that that scene belonged in the later part. Once, on page 36, "Lydgate's anguish. Rosamond's repulsion" (now part of chapter 75) was included in the plans for Book 7. Once, too, on page 37 under "Conclusion of Part VII" but separated from the rest of the items, is the entry, "Query: connexion of Will's return."

This last item, once the "*Course of Part VII*" on page 38 was established (and the part written?), became a major source of concern to George Eliot in her planning of Book 8. Had she carried out her original intention of continuing the Will-Dorothea story in Book 7 immediately following their second farewell scene at the end of Book 6, there would have been no need for Will to leave Middlemarch at all: he could have said goodbye to Dorothea and gone to Rosamond, presumably to say goodbye, and been seen there by Dorothea "in emotion" etc. But now the scene at the end of Book 6 is followed by the Raffles episode and the scandal, so Will must leave for a while—he has already said goodbye twice without leaving—and therefore some reason for his return and the relation of his return to the other events must be taken into account. These considerations are evident on page 39 of the notebook: the first of the "Conditions" listed on that page is "Return of Will Ladislaw: reasons for his return. Time at which it happens," and on the same page his return is related chronologically to the events of the Raffles-Bulstrode-Lydgate plot in a list of "Times":

> The death of Raffles about 21st. March
> Bambridge's return 26th.
> Meeting of Sanitary Reform, April 10th.
> Return of Will Ladislaw

Why Will returns evidently still concerned the author on page 40 of the notebook: "Will Ladislaw's arrival & its causes." More important, however, now that his return occurs after the scandal, it is related to that event in more than mere chronology. In the novel, the scandal drives the wedge between Dorothea and Will still deeper by making his rather unacceptable origins known to all Middlemarch; the scandal also drives

Rosamond to despair and thus occasions her throwing herself upon Ladislaw. His motive for returning—to observe whether it is moral to use Bulstrode's debt to him as a means of obtaining money from the banker for the founding of a colony—is extremely thin, and it is saved only by the fact that Will and even Lydgate realize that it is only a pretext for Will's seeing Dorothea once again.

Other aspects of the Will-Dorothea story and its relation to the Lydgate-Rosamond situation were reworked after Book 7 had been completed. In *Quarry II*, 40, the events of the last part of *Middlemarch* were drawn up in this fashion:

1 Dorothea & Lydgate
2 Dorothea goes to deliver a letter at Lydgate's
  Finds Will Ladislaw there. Suspicions confirmed by their emotion.

---

1 Reasons why Dorothea does not immediately have her interview with Lydgate.
3 Mrs. Bulstrode made aware of the Facts about her husband.
  Their final arrangements. Fred Vincy.[19]
  Lydgate's misery (written in above: & gloom). Rosamond's repulsion.
3 Lydgate's outpouring to Dorothea. She takes the money to free him, & finds Will Ladislaw with Dorothea [*sic*].
  She goes away with the impression that they are lovers.
  Her emotions of jealousy: making her more distinctly aware of her love.
  Her struggle to overcome her selfish feeling. She goes again to R.
  Will's outburst to Rosamond after Dorothea is gone away: cutting to the quick.
    When Dorothea comes again to Rosamond with love, Rosamond is wrought upon to tell her that Will loves Dorothea alone.

This is followed on page 41 by a single entry, the only line on the page: " Dorothea's motive in going to Rosamond."

This plan for Book 8 plunges in immediately with the Dorothea-Lydgate scene listed several times among the plans for Book 7, and leads from that scene directly to Dorothea's discovery of Will and Rosamond together. But then George Eliot drew a line across the page and began the new plan with the postponement of the Dorothea-Lydgate scene. This postponement in fact takes place in chapter 72, when Mr. Farebrother, joined by Sir James and Mr. Brooke, points out the delicacy of Lydgate's case, the limits of possible action, and the caution necessary in bringing up the subject to Lydgate. The third item in this new plan— " Lydgate's misery. Rosamond's repulsion "—is in the novel split into two chapters, 73 and 75, one before and one after Mrs. Bulstrode's becoming aware of her husband's part in the scandal, all three of which items have

---

[19] George Eliot enclosed this line in square brackets, apparently when she realized it was to come later in the part.

at one time or another been part of the plans for Book 7. In the list, Will's arrival precedes the long planned-for Lydgate-Dorothea scene, and so is slightly out of place. After Lydgate speaks to Dorothea in both the novel (chap. 76) and in these plans, the events of the Rosamond-Will-Dorothea triangle take place.

The preparation for these events and even some of the changes in the events and their sequence have been dealt with above, but now the whole development and change can be summarized.

The events of the Rosamond-Will-Dorothea triangle had many forms in the notebook. There is no hint of them until the " *Will Ladislaw &* *Dorothea* " summary on page 27, since, as recently as page 24, George Eliot was content with the uncomplicated entry, " Second marriage of Dorothea." In that summary, Dorothea, upon discovering Will and Rosamond together, breaks out with " anger, jealousy, reproach," and vows never to marry Will. In the " Scenes " on pages 29-30, there is also no hint that Will has left Middlemarch and returned; Dorothea discovers him and Rosamond together and bursts out in the same manner; Will, it is clear here, leaves and comes back to Rosamond to reproach her; Dorothea leaves, returns, and is told the truth, etc. In " Sketch 2," pages 32-34, for the first time Dorothea's motives in going to Lydgate's—the loan and her wish to advise Rosamond—are clear. Here Dorothea does not upbraid Will. He leaves the scene, and Dorothea, " repressing her anguish, carries out her intended admonition, & quits Rosamond." For the first time on page 40, it is Dorothea alone who goes away. Also on that page for the first time is the material which is to make up chapter 80: Dorothea's " Struggle to overcome her selfish feeling," only after which she " goes again to R." Then, though out of sequence, comes Will's reproach of Rosamond, this time not after he has left and returned, but after " Dorothea is gone away." Finally, the desired end of the episode, toward which all this has been working—Rosamond's confession to Dorothea that Will loves only Dorothea—appears again. On page 41 the entry—" Dorothea's motive in going to Rosamond "—probably refers to the first visit, which had now been given motivation in terms borne out in the novel (" She takes the money to free him ") but which still apparently caused George Eliot some uneasiness.

In this part there are three chapters—74, 85, and 86—which do not directly concern the Lydgate-Rosamond-Will-Dorothea portion of the plot. In the first of these, Mrs. Bulstrode learns of the scandal concerning her husband; in the second, Bulstrode proposes leaving Stone Court to the management of Fred Vincy, and in the last, Garth breaks the good news to Mary and she to Fred, making their immediate marriage possible. Under " Motives (in general) " on page 11, indented beneath " Blight on Bulstrode & Lydgate," is the queried item, "Action of Caleb Garth & Mr. Farebrother." Whether the action of Garth refers to his part in Bulstrode's disposal of Stone Court or to his actions after Raffles tells him Bulstrode's secret is uncertain; at any rate, these items were apparently added to this list long after the list itself had been drawn up. The first concrete item, therefore, which refers to one of these three chapters appears as item *eta* on page 33: "Mrs. Bulstrode," which, coming as it does in a list concerning the scandal and its aftermath, obviously refers to her learning of the scandal or to her reactions to it. On page 37, under "Conclusion of Part VII," there is another reference to this incident: "[Bulstrode] returns home finds Mrs. Bulstrode partly informed: on Lydgate." But in the novel at this point Mrs. Bulstrode knows nothing, not even about Lydgate. The notes headed "Part VIII" on page 40 merely state: "Mrs. Bulstrode made aware of the Facts about her husband." This is accurate as a summary, and, coming after the postponement of Dorothea's interview with Lydgate and before that interview takes place, it is accurate in indicating the sequence of these events. But how poor a note it is for that magnificent chapter (74), one of the finest scenes in *Middlemarch* or in any other novel, in which Mrs. Bulstrode's "friends" discuss her plight, hint to her of the difficulty until she rushes to her brother (Mr. Vincy) to learn the truth, and then, after a struggle with which we have much more sympathy, it seems to me, than we do with Dorothea's struggle after the scene at Lydgate's, she emerges solemnly and gently to stand at her husband's side. In this scene a character who has hardly been mentioned in *Middlemarch* up to this point except, ironically, to bring to the attention of Rosamond and Lydgate before their marriage the force of the Middlemarch scandal about their relationship, suddenly emerges to remain indelibly in the reader's mind.

The first note concerning the two later chapters, 85 and 86, does not appear until *Quarry II*, 39, headed "Conditions": "What becomes of Bulstrode's arrangements as to property, especially Stone Court?" and "How Fred & Mary get married." The question seems rhetorical, George Eliot apparently intending Fred to get Stone Court all along and simply noting here that this was one of the "Conditions" in this last part of *Middlemarch* which she had to present. Once again, it seems, George Eliot knew where it was she wanted her story to go, but was uncertain as to the route and timing. In *Quarry II*, 40, a page headed "Part VIII," where most of the plans for this part reached just about their final form, the disposition of Bulstrode's property immediately follows Mrs. Bulstrode's consciousness of the scandal—"Mrs. Bulstrode made aware of the Facts about her husband./ Their final arrangements. Fred Vincy"—a sequence which would have placed this material approximately in chapter 75. But the last part of the entry was enclosed in brackets, indicating that George Eliot changed her mind about the relative position of these arrangements and decided to hold them off until the last chapter or so of the novel.

All of these plans for the Lydgate-Rosamond-Will-Dorothea and the Bulstrode-Garth-Vincy plot lines (N. B. how the plot-line designations themselves reveal the extent to which the "Miss Brooke" and "Middlemarch" stories have been integrated and realigned within the larger *Middlemarch*) result, on the last page of the notebook, *Quarry II*, 42, in a list of twelve items which represent the final stage in the planning of Book 8 before the actual writing of the part began:

1 Dorothea wants to help Lydgate & is checked
2 Lydgate's first anguish under the sense of his position
3 Mrs. Bulstrode learns her sorrow
4 Rosamond's behavior & Lydgate's towards her
5 Lydgate tells Dorothea
6 Dorothea goes to see Rosamond & take (the £1000) money for Lydgate. Finds Will with Rosamond.
7 Will's outburst of bitterness against R.
8 Dorothea's anguish & struggles. She goes to Rosamond again who tells her about Will's truth.
9 Will's interview with Dorothea: Reconciliation
10 The Garths & Fred Vincy.
11 Dorothea tells her uncle & the Chettams that she is going to marry Will
12 Mr. Brooke will be father at the wedding but as a corrective proposes to cut off the entail

Finale

The first seven of these items accurately summarize the nature and sequence of the first seven chapters of Book 8, chapters 72-78. The last of these chapters was split up in the novel to make chapter 79. The list of chapters in this part on page 15 of *Quarry II* has been corrected to include this seventy-ninth chapter, which it designates as "Will & Lydgate," but this list on page 42 is uncorrected, another indication that the list on page 42 is earlier than the one on page 15 despite their positions in the *Quarry*. Item 8 in this list became two chapters, 80 and 81, both in the novel and in the list on page 15. The next chapter in the novel, 82, listed on page 15 simply as "Will Ladislaw," tells of Will's reasons for returning to Middlemarch, of his actions after he berated Rosamond, and of his taking the coach to Riverton but returning to the Lydgate home to hear from Rosamond that she had told Dorothea the truth. All this was omitted from the list on page 42. Item 9 of that list thus appears as the eleventh chapter of Book 8. Too, the sequence of the next three items in the list is somewhat different in the novel: item 10 appears as chapter 86, the last of the novel (or, if this item can be considered to include the discussion between Bulstrode and his wife about the disposition of Stone Court which is not in the list at all, this item includes both chapters 85 and 86) ; items 11 and 12 both appear in chapter 84, though, contrary to item 11, it is not Dorothea who tells Sir James of her intention to marry Will (as also indicated earlier in " Scenes," p. 30), but Mr. Brooke who carries the news. The list in *Quarry II*, 42, though fuller in detail is less accurate both as to the exact nature and as to the exact sequence of the events in Book 8 of *Middlemarch* than is the sketchier, more hastily written list in *Quarry II*, 15. The former was undoubtedly the last sketch of the part before it was written, or at least before it was completed, whereas the list on page 15 noted the completion of each chapter as it was finished.

The pattern for the composition of Book 8 of *Middlemarch* is much the same as that for the composition of Books 5-7. The main events in the part, in this case those surrounding Dorothea, Will, and Rosamond, had been known to the author for some time, but their relative position and interrelationship were not clear until late in the planning stage. In this case, indeed, for some time, even perhaps up to the time at which George Eliot completed Book 6, she intended the events of Book 8 for Book 7 and vice versa. Once she established the proper sequence of these main events, they began to fall into parts. Even so, she intended some of the events which now appear in Book 8—e. g., Lydgate's conversation with Dorothea, Rosamond's reaction to the scandal surrounding her husband, and Mrs. Bulstrode's learning of the scandal—for Book 7. When she completed Book 7, she saw that these events were left for Book 8 and that she had to work them into that part. At this late stage, with Book 7 already written and Book 8 being planned, the course of the major events was still undergoing change, e. g., the postponement of the Lydgate-Dorothea conversation, the action of Dorothea upon finding Will and Rosamond alone together. Perhaps more for this part than for the others, many of the plans involved motives and arrangements, e. g., Dorothea's motive in going to Rosamond, Will's in returning to Middlemarch, and the disposition of Stone Court and Dorothea's income. Finally, we see once again, that even after she had completed her plans, while she was writing the very words of the chapters themselves, George Eliot felt free to change not only the sequence of events and the relationships involved, but even the details of the action, and she felt free too to add details, situations, and relationships which she had not foreseen in her plans, e. g., in chapter 79, the Will-Lydgate scene; in chapter 84, Mr. Brooke, rather than Dorothea, telling Sir James of her intention to marry.

7.

When, after the first two and one-half months of 1871, George Eliot finished joining " Middlemarch " to " Miss Brooke," she had nineteen chapters of the new *Middlemarch*, made up of chapters from " Miss Brooke," perhaps some fragments of " Middlemarch," a great deal of rewritten material, and some new material. In May, Lewes proposed that the novel be published in eight bimonthly half-volume parts, the purpose of the suggestion being to stimulate sales and profits (those of *Felix Holt*, considering the stature of George Eliot among contemporary novelists, having been disappointing, at least to the publisher who paid her £5,000 for the rights) and to accommodate the peculiar length and form which *Middlemarch* seemed to be taking, i. e., seeming to require four volumes and being made up so far of two distinct and almost independent stories. During the summer months of 1871 the plan was accepted by the publisher, who had read the first two parts and agreed that they fit the plan since they were in fact almost independent. During that period, George Eliot was writing the third part, apparently still with the idea in mind of independent bimonthly parts; but in Book 3, despite the plan, the various strands of the story were all present. Book 3 was completed in the fall and Book 4 begun. By winter, however, the wisdom of the plan for independent parts became dubious, and chapters from Books 2 and 3 were transposed so as to include elements from " Miss Brooke " and elements from " Middlemarch " in each part. Meanwhile, hampered by illness, George Eliot was not making satisfactory progress on Book 4, since less than half of that part had been written before Christmas of 1871. But, she consoled herself, she was working on " construction, which, once done, serves as good wheels for progress."

In *Quarry II*, 9, in a list headed " Motives," are the first results of this " construction." The items in this list apply chiefly to Book 4 and to a lesser extent to Book 5. There are no comparable notes for any of the first three parts, but from this point on there are even more extensive plans for the later parts of *Middlemarch*, plans which, as the novel progressed, got more and more detailed. It was with these notes and plans, clarified or supplemented by evidence in the manuscript, that this chapter was chiefly concerned. From the study and analysis of these notebook plans certain conclusions have been reached about both the changes in the course and specific nature of *Middlemarch* which took place between the time the fictional events were first planned and the time they were written, and about the manner in which George Eliot worked, i. e., how she went about writing *Middlemarch*.

One of the things revealed in the notebook is that George Eliot had a good idea of what the major events in the novel were to be quite early in the writing of the novel; in the list of " Private dates " in *Quarry II*, 4, certainly drawn up in 1871, most of these major events appear: Celia's and Lydgate's marriages, Dorothea's second marriage, the deaths of Featherstone, Casaubon, and Raffles, Brooke's standing for Parliament, and Bulstrode's purchase of Stone Court. The only major events not included are Lydgate's accumulation of debt, the "bribe," and the scandal following the death of Raffles, and Fred Vincy's choice of a career, final attainment of Stone Court, and marriage to Mary Garth; their absence, however, does not necessarily mean George Eliot did not foresee them at this time. The only event in the list which does not come to pass in the novel is the birth of Rosamond's baby; that birth becomes, in *Middlemarch*, a miscarriage brought on by Rosamond's vanity and stubbornness and is a brilliant stroke in depicting her shallow, willful character. To say that George Eliot knew what major events were to be in her novel, however, is not to claim that even the broadest outline of *Middlemarch* was in George Eliot's mind or notes at this time, for it is as necessary to know the sequence as it is the nature of events in order to construct an outline, and more than half of the dates in the list were changed before the events they concern appeared in the novel, and, in several cases, not only the dates but the relative sequence of events was altered, e. g., the sequence of Celia's marriage and Featherstone's death, the birth of Celia's baby and Casaubon's death, Dorothea's second marriage and Raffles' death.[20] And, though absence of a major event or situation from this list is not proof that it was not foreseen at this time, neither is it proof that it was: it is particularly doubtful, for example, whether at this stage George Eliot knew what the relationship between Bulstrode's past and Will's history was to be.

Plans for Books 4 and 5 in the notebook are rather scanty, but, by a judicious use of hindsight, we find they reveal almost the same pattern as the more copious plans for the later parts. George Eliot, during the early planning stage of each part, had in mind the major events of the part but neither the sequence of those events nor the relationships among them, nor did she have a very clear idea of the point at which the part being planned was to end.

Plans for the last three parts are much more extensive and consequently reveal a little more about the way in which each part developed under the author's hand. She usually summarized the major plot lines

[20] For a discussion of the chronology of *Middlemarch*, see chapter 2 of my doctoral dissertation, "*Middlemarch* from Notebook to Novel: A Study of George Eliot's Creative Method" (Urbana, 1956).

separately and without regard to interrelationships, e. g., " *Will Ladislaw & Dorothea* " (p. 27) , " Bulstrode & Raffles " (p. 28) , and " Sketch 2," concerning Will, Dorothea, and Rosamond (p. 32) . These fuller plans also reveal the attention George Eliot paid to events, motives, and situations which, though they do not form chapters or sequences themselves, underlie the main action of the novel, e. g., the six-page sketch of Bulstrode's past (pp. 17-22) , the " Conditions " (p. 39) , and such scattered items as " Query: connexion of Will's return " (p. 37) , " Dorothea's motive in going to Rosamond " (p. 41) , etc. These plans also reveal, more clearly than do the scantier plans for Books 4 and 5, that the major events were clear to the author long before she wrote them into chapters, and the sequences and relationships were not too clear even in the later stages of planning.

Though the notebook reveals no startling changes in the plan of the novel, many small but telling touches, like that of Rosamond's miscarriage, were added either as the plans developed or after the plans had been made, while George Eliot was engaged in writing the chapters themselves. Among these additions, which were either not prepared for at all or not prepared long in advance of writing, are many of the very scenes which make *Middlemarch* so magnificent a novel. Rosamond's miscarriage, brought on by her own character, is only one instance of how the Lydgate-Rosamond story is deepened far beyond anything suggested in the plans. That chapter in which Lydgate's plight is seen through the eyes of Mr. Farebrother, who, sympathetic as he is, cannot see in the pretty Rosamond the character which makes the plight more difficult to bear, chapter 63, is nowhere suggested in the early plans of this part, appearing only once in the notebook (" *Course of Part VII,*" p. 38) , so late in the planning of Book 7 that the chapter itself may already have been written. The next chapter too, the aggravating and powerful incident of the house-letting, appears for the first time in this late plan and may have been written before it was noted in the *Quarry*.

Similarly, though the notebook makes provisions for a scene in which Mrs. Bulstrode is informed of the scandal affecting her husband, at first it was to occur immediately after the " Sanitary Reform " meeting (itself changed from a vestry meeting and thereby given plot significance by darkening the threat of cholera) , and she was to have had knowledge of Lydgate's part in the scandal (nowhere is it suggested in the notebook that Lydgate, as physician and warmhearted man, goes to the side of the stricken Bulstrode even as the scandal falls about the banker's head) . Another passage in the novel which was apparently intended as a high point but with which most modern readers have perhaps less sympathy— the sequence in which Dorothea discovers Will and Rosamond together, leaves, struggles with herself and returns, while Will berates Rosamond—had been changed considerably within the planning stages. In one plan Dorothea was to have made a passionate declaration of her love for Will at the time of the discovery and announced her decision never to marry him; Will was to have left and to have returned for his scene with Rosamond. Dorothea now retains her dignity and control; Will blows up on the spot after Dorothea leaves. Finally, a touch was added in the later stages of *Middlemarch*, which constitutes a change from the notebook and which has no cosmic significance but which brilliantly adds to the "realization" of time, place, and character, and by this realization unites or pulls together different aspects of the novel; Dorothea, according to the plan, was to have told Sir James of her decision to marry Will Ladislaw; now, in chapter 84, it is her uncle who makes the revelation. When Brooke appears in this scene his sadness is attributed by the anti-Reform Cadwalladers and Chettam to the news that the House of Lords has thrown out the Reform Bill. But the bad news is not only political; Brooke divulges in his characteristic roundabout manner the personal "bad" news about Dorothea.

Relatively minor changes such as this one and relatively minor changes in sequence and relationship are visible in every part, almost chapter by chapter. It is indeed in such changes that the notebook is most revealing. The net result of those changes is usually a more tightly knit novel, one part of the story, one situation and incident leading into, affecting, resulting in, other parts of the story, other incidents. These changes have been presented at some length above and are too numerous to repeat here. Perhaps the chief of the changes of sequence may be recalled, however: the reversing of the order of Dorothea's second marriage and the scandal involving Lydgate and Bulstrode, the latter of which was to have followed the former. By reversing the sequence of these actions George Eliot set up a whole new series of relationships between the Lydgates and those who are to be the Ladislaws. Dorothea, after the scandal, is aroused to the defense of Lydgate. Her belief in him spurs him to reveal to her the galling nature of his marriage. To help him out of his debt to Bulstrode and to advise Rosamond of her husband's innocence, Dorothea goes to see her. With the knowledge that the Lydgate marriage is a little less than ideal, with the hints dropped by Mrs. Cadwallader at the behest of Sir James,[21] with her own memory of a previous visit to the

---

[21] Why is it that critics of *Middlemarch* devote so little attention to Sir James? Do they believe that his horror at the thought of Dorothea's remarrying, and in particular his horror at the prospect of her marrying Ladislaw, that the violence of his suggestions to separate them and the means to which he eventually stoops—having Mrs. Cadwallader spread the gossip concerning Will and Rosamond—are motivated by

Lydgate home where she heard singing and found Will and Rosamond alone together, Dorothea is prepared to misinterpret the emotional scene between Rosamond and Will that she sees upon entering the Lydgate drawing room. Had she and Will been married before the scandal, as the author had originally planned, it is difficult to see how all this would have been brought about.

The notebook thus reveals how George Eliot's plans for *Middlemarch* changed and grew, how the major incidents were ordered and surrounded by organic, interrelating, "realizing" events, and how the events became scenes, the scenes chapters, and the chapters parts. It reveals more. Even a cursory examination of the final plan for each part (remembering that the chapter-by-chapter lists of the parts on pages 5-7, 10, and 12-15 are *not* plans but statements or records of finished chapters) and a comparison of these last plans with the pertinent part of *Middlemarch* itself reveals how many changes and how great were the changes and additions made during the actual writing of the chapters. The greatest "planning" stage was the writing itself, George Eliot treating her notebook not as a blueprint to be followed to the letter, but as a steppingstone in her progress toward the completed novel.

This does not mean that the manuscript of *Middlemarch* should be expected to reveal great and sweeping changes, vast shifts, additions of whole chapters, or thoroughgoing revisions. Indeed, after the transposition of blocks of chapters in Books 2 and 3 discussed earlier, there was only one shift in the sequence of chapters, insofar as the manuscript pagination can be relied upon to reveal such a shift. There are, too, several additions of minor scenes made after the chapter in which they now appear was completed (e. g., the scene in chapter 24 in which Fred arrives at the Garth home to confess his inability to pay the debt) and signs in the manuscript that a few pages, but only a few at any one time, have been rewritten. No vast shifts and changes, then, should be expected. What the manuscript reveals instead is that writing, to George Eliot, was indeed a process, that changes in wording, phrasing, detail, and image were made on every page, that *Middlemarch* grew in her mind and before her eyes on the page she was writing.

Middlemarch, however, is too vast a novel, and—since George Eliot made on the average four or five changes on each of the twelve hundred

---

his concern for the family reputation, or by his dislike (shared by many of the critics themselves) of Ladislaw? Is there not a strong suggestion that Sir James, an unsuccessful suitor for Dorothea's hand before her first marriage, still has more than a brotherly affection for her? Is it possible that after Casaubon's death he regrets his marriage to Dorothea's sister which took place when Dorothea, married to the scholar, seemed hopelessly beyond his reach?

or so pages of manuscript—the number of changes is too great for one to make a definitive study of all the revisions in the novel (at least until the first step, publication of a variorum edition of the novel, is taken). Instead, the next chapter analyzes in detail the revisions in the manuscript of a single chapter of *Middlemarch*.

The chapter chosen, chapter 81, comes very late in the novel, well beyond the fusion of "Miss Brooke" and "Middlemarch," and so may be considered a truly *Middlemarch* chapter. It had been prepared for by careful planning in the notebook. It was rather extensively revised. But it is chosen for more than just these reasons, for more than its typicality. For it is tempting to conclude from what has been said above about the writing stage as a process that the notebook plans are the result of conscious planning and that the changes made during the writing process are the result of unconscious "inspiration." Indeed, George Eliot thought that the best of her writing was done more or less unconsciously. And she singled out chapter 81 as an example of unconscious writing. Changes made during the writing process, however, are just as conscious, just as much a product of the intellect as are the plans of the notebook—*just as much*: that is to say, notebook plans too are sometimes the result of sudden insights, sudden intuitions, but there, as in the writing process itself, the author's judgment still functions and can accept or reject these flashes at will. It is not the intent of this study to deny the importance of the unconscious in the creative process but simply to show that it rarely operates in and of itself to the exclusion of the conscious control of the author, and that the whole process of creation is much more complex than the black-white terminology of "conscious" and "unconscious" can comprehend.

CHAPTER FOUR

The Writing of Chapter 81

In the previous chapter it was pointed out that there are frequently considerable differences between George Eliot's final notebook plans and the text of *Middlemarch*, differences which evidently resulted from changes and additions she made while writing. For writing to her was a process: the act of embodying skeletal notebook plans in the flesh of fiction acted upon her and suggested to her expressions and events she could not have foreseen. The act of writing was thus truly the last stage of planning.

Because these changes seem to have been unpremeditated and unplanned, there is a tendency to identify their origin as different in kind from that of the notebook plans, even though the plans themselves often had to "occur to" the author in some way other than through ratiocination. Critics and writers alike, however, often identify writing with the unconscious and planning with the conscious.

In the nineteenth century it was particularly comfortable to identify creation with the unconscious, though the terms used were somewhat different: nineteenth-century critics and writers spoke of "inspiration," "possession," or even "imagination" in contexts in which we might use "the unconscious." This faculty—if we admit that it is a separate and separable faculty—is of course present in the act of composition, but also present for most writers at most times is judgment, an aspect of the conscious mind. The heirs of romanticism in the nineteenth and twentieth centuries tend to undervalue judgment, even to deny it a place in the creation of art. They therefore start with the truism that an "idea" or an "expression" must begin somewhere, must suggest itself to the artist at some point or other, and exaggerate this truism into an aesthetic. Inspiration, the unconscious, or the emotive becomes all that is good in the creative process; judgment, the conscious, or the intellect all that is bad. Critics sometimes identify what they approve of in a work as the product of the unconscious, what they disapprove of as the product of the conscious mind (calculation). Writers, humanly anxious to be thought inhumanly great, magnify the unconscious element in their work. Their best work, they say, was written without premeditation, in a frenzy of inspiration. Therefore it follows, they believe, that revision and hard work are the signs of those who are less than geniuses. They try to play down, even to deny, that aspect of their effort; at their best, they say, they not only wrote while at a pitch of inspiration, but they did not have to revise (for surely the conscious mind cannot presume to judge the product of that superior faculty, the unconscious).

George Eliot seems to have labored under such nineteenth-century notions. According to what she told John Cross, she wrote in the manner prescribed for geniuses, in a fit of inspiration and without revising. Chapter 81 of *Middlemarch* was written in this way, she specified, and thus was typical of her creative method when she was doing her best work. There is no reason to believe this chapter was not written in a fashion typical of George Eliot's creative method, and since the manuscript of the chapter is extant, it should show traces of that method. These traces will be described below.

In 1880, about eight years after she had written chapter 81 of *Middlemarch*, George Eliot allegedly described how she had written it to John Cross, then her husband. He reported it thus in the *Life*:

During our short married life . . . George Eliot wrote very little, so that I have but slight personal experience of how the creative effort affected her. But she told me that, in all that she considered her best writing, there was a " not herself " which took possession of her, and that she felt her own personality to be merely the instrument through which this spirit, as it were, was acting. Particularly she dwelt on this in regard to the scene in " Middlemarch " between Dorothea and Rosamond, saying that, although she always knew they had, sooner or later, to come together, she kept the idea resolutely out of her mind until Dorothea was in Rosamond's drawing-room. Then, abandoning herself to the inspiration of the moment, she wrote the whole scene exactly as it stands, without alteration or erasure, in an intense state of excitement and agitation, feeling herself entirely possessed by the feelings of the two women (3: 424-25).

Though this is the only reference to the composition of this chapter, it is not the only reference to George Eliot's creative process made on apparently good authority. In *Blackwood's Magazine* for February, 1881, in an obituary article presumably by William Blackwood, nephew of John, George Eliot's creative process was described from a publisher's point of view:

George Eliot was the most careful and accurate among authors. Her beautifully written manuscript, free from blur or erasure, and with every letter delicately and distinctly finished, was only the outward and visible sign of the inward labour which she had taken to work out her ideas. She never drew any of her facts or impressions from second-hand; and thus, in spite of the number and variety of her illustrations, she had rarely much to correct in her proof-sheets (p. 267).

Since much of what the author narrated in this article concerned the relationship between George Eliot and John Blackwood, he must have had access to the correspondence between these two, and it is probably on this correspondence that his impression of the way George Eliot wrote was based. One triangular exchange of letters in particular concerned George Eliot's creative method. In the fall of 1874, John Blackwood wrote Alexander Kinglake, author of *Invasion of Crimea*, this description of that method:

George Eliot . . . tells me a large slice of Manuscript [of *Daniel Deronda*] has passed into the "irrevocable." She thinks and thinks over what she is going to write. It "simmers" in her mind as she says and then when she puts it upon paper it seems to pass into reality not to be altered.[1]

On November 19, Blackwood then wrote to George Eliot quoting Kinglake's response:

"What you tell me of the intellectual fermentation from which works like *Middlemarch* result is very interesting and makes me envy the process of disciplined thought which after the 'simmering' passes all at once into 'the irrevocable.' "

We thus have rather different versions of how George Eliot wrote her novels. The aesthetic and worshipping Cross, or George Eliot herself, would have us believe that she created in an almost Platonic frenzy, that at least her best welled up from what we would call the unconscious, without planning and without revision. The practical and craftsmanlike William Blackwood, on the other hand, would have us believe that George Eliot carefully and consciously worked out not only what she was going to say but the way in which she was going to say it before committing herself to paper. John Blackwood seems to suggest to Kinglake, though the publisher does not himself say it, that her words passed " *all at once* " into " the irrevocable," into their final form. Cross admits no planning in George Eliot's " best "; the Blackwoods emphasize the careful planning. Both would seem to agree that in the act of writing itself there was little conscious control. Cross and William Blackwood agree that, at least in her " best," George Eliot made no revisions in manuscript.

Cross's remark, both because it allegedly came from George Eliot herself and because his book has been the chief source of details about

---

[1] I am indebted to Wing Commander G. D. Blackwood for a copy of this letter, which is not in the *Letters*. Blackwood apparently based his summary on a letter from George Eliot dated 5 Nov. 1873—" I am slowly simmering towards another big book " and on an 11 Nov. 1874 letter whose absence Haight notes (*Letters* 6: 91, n. 1) but which is to be found in the National Library of Scotland—" the thick slice of manuscript which had passed into the irrevocable "—as well as on references in the long correspondence between them and, no doubt, on many conversations they had through the years of their friendship. See my article, " ' Into the Irrevocable ': A New George Eliot Letter," *JEGP*, 57 (October, 1958), 704-7.

George Eliot's life and opinions, has naturally had more currency. It is no wonder, then, that Mrs. Bennett (pp. 168-69) ,[2] praising the Dorothea-Rosamond scene in chapter 81 of *Middlemarch* as, " the most brilliant stroke of creative genius " in the presentation of Rosamond's character, quotes the above passage from Cross in order to demonstrate " how little . . . that scene was consciously contrived," how " George Eliot had abandoned conscious intellectual control " in writing it. Much of Mrs. Bennett's book, in fact, consists in distinguishing those passages which are " conscious," " contrived," or " intellectual " from those which are " unconscious," " spontaneous," " emotional," or " imaginative "—within each of these groups the terms are used interchangeably. Such terms as " conscious " and " unconscious " and " contrived " and " spontaneous " when used by a critic are ambiguous: they characterize both the *effect* of a passage on the reader and *the method of composition*. Mrs. Bennett's authority for identifying the effects of various passages is her own fine critical sensibility. Her authority for identifying the method of composition is only Cross's report of his conversation with his wife.

Let us examine Cross's statement. He described George Eliot's method of composition (when she was at her best) as a single-stage process: she wrote not only without planning and without revision after she had written, but without any alteration or erasure even while she was writing. The lack of revision, in fact, is the sign of how unconsciously she wrote. We have seen in the previous chapter that there was, indeed, a large gulf at times between the last plans in the notebook and the finished chapters in *Middlemarch*. But no matter how they differed from the text, there were plans, and plenty of them. The *Quarries*, then, would seem to contradict Cross, but in order to disprove his statement completely we would have to know just what George Eliot " considered her best writing " and prove that *that* was planned, for it is only this writing which Cross claimed was unplanned. The one scene Cross reported George Eliot as identifying not only as her best, but specifically as one of those best parts which she wrote while " possessed," is contained in chapter 81 of *Middlemarch*. We have traced some of the notebook plans into the novel in the previous chapter and have dealt both with Book 8 in which chapter 81 appears and with the specific series of chapters involving Will, Dorothea, and Rosamond. But let us now pay particular attention to the plans for chapter 81 and the events leading up to it with the Cross statement in mind.

George Eliot " always knew they [Dorothea and Rosamond] had sooner or later to come together, [but] she kept the idea resolutely out of her

[2] Joan Bennett, *George Eliot: Her Mind and Her Art* (Cambridge, 1948) .

mind until Dorothea was in Rosamond's drawing-room." *Quarry II* for *Middlemarch* unfortunately indicates that this just is not true.

In chapter 77 Dorothea has found Rosamond and Will alone together in an obviously emotional situation. She has been prepared to suspect a love affair between the two by her own observation, by gossip, and by ambiguous statements from Will and Lydgate. She leaves, and in leaving is noticed for the first time by Will and Rosamond. In chapter 78 Will lashes out at Rosamond for ruining whatever good opinion Dorothea, the only woman he ever loved, held of him. In chapter 80 Dorothea wrestles all night with her jealousy and overcomes it, deciding to return to Rosamond and complete the errand she set out to do the day before, i. e., to advise Rosamond of Lydgate's innocence of wrongdoing in the Raffles affair. In chapter 81 Dorothea once more enters the Lydgate drawing room, and Rosamond, when she discovers that Dorothea has not come to upbraid her but to help her, is overcome, and, uncharacteristically unselfish, tells Dorothea that yesterday's scene was her (Rosamond's) fault and that Will loves only Dorothea.

In *Quarry II*, 11, under "Motives (in general)," there is the entry, "Rosamond's flirtation with Ladislaw," followed by a queried entry, "? Dorothea after severe struggle goes to Rosamond." This is the first indication in the notebook of a scene similar to the one in chapter 81; indeed, because these entries come so early in the planning of the last parts of *Middlemarch*, too early for actual scenes to be prepared, they appear to be later additions to that list. There is no hint of such a scene in the list of "Elements" on page 24, the "Second marriage of Dorothea" having been listed without amplification. But in the summary on page 27 ("*Will Ladislaw & Dorothea*," written during the planning and composition of Book 6) after Dorothea "finds him [Will] with Mrs. Lydgate. Scene between her & Will—anger, jealousy, reproach, ending in Dorothea's passionate avowal, & declaration that she will never marry him. Will reproaches Rosamond with having ruined his happiness. Rosamond alarmed lest Dorothea should tell Lydgate," there is a brief summary of the matter of chapter 81: "Dorothea goes to R. having conquered her jealousy by pity, & hears that Will has been true to her." This entry was made apparently before George Eliot had completed Book 6. In the list of "Scenes" on pages 29-30, also apparently made up before Book 6 was completed, items 12-15 present the material of chapters 77 and 78 in much the same way as the summary, and item 16 presents the material of chapter 81: "Dorothea, wrought on by compassion, goes to Rosamond, & so moves her that R. tells D. how Will has been true." This adds to the summary the fact that Dorothea "moves" Rosamond, without mentioning that Rosamond fears Dorothea will tell Lydgate of the episode with Will; thus it brings the scene closer to the finished version. On page 34, in a continuation of " Sketch 2 " (which was begun on page 32) written during the period when the Will-Dorothea situation was still intended for Book 7, these events were again summarized, though here it is Will who leaves the scene and Dorothea, " repressing her anguish, carries out her intended admonition, & quits Rosamond." On page 40, under the heading " Part VIII," the Raffles affair having already assumed its final location in Book 7, George Eliot again summarized the events which were to make up chapters 77-80 and made two entries having to do with chapter 81: " Her [Dorothea's] struggle to overcome her selfish feeling [80]. She goes again to R." and, " When Dorothea comes again to Rosamond with love, Rosamond is wrought upon to tell her that Will loves Dorothea alone." On page 41 there is but one entry, " Dorothea's motive in going to Rosamond," which entry may pertain either to her first visit or to her return. Finally, in what was apparently the final plan of this last part and the last page of the notebook (p. 42), a twelve-item list headed " Part VIII " contains as item 8, " Dorothea's anguish & struggles. She goes to Rosamond again who tells her about Will's truth."

Such were the plans for the preparation and presentation of chapter 81. Preparations for this scene underwent some changes: at first Dorothea upon discovering Will and Rosamond together was to give vent to her anger, declare her love for Will, but vow not to marry him, a plan which persisted through the " Scenes." In " Sketch 2 " George Eliot decided to have Dorothea repress " her anguish " and continue with her mission to Rosamond, Will having left. Both these plans would have presented the Dorothea-Rosamond scene immediately following Dorothea's discovery, now in chapter 77. Finally, on page 40, it is Dorothea who goes away, Will who " blows up " at Rosamond, and Dorothea, after a struggle, who returns to carry out her original mission, thus necessitating a second scene in the Lydgate drawing room, a direct scene between Dorothea and Rosamond alone. This scene, besides taking place upon Dorothea's return rather than immediately after her discovery of Will and Rosamond together, changes slightly in its nature: there is a growing awareness in the plans that Rosamond confesses because she is " wrought upon " by Dorothea, rather than because she fears that Dorothea will tell Lydgate of the episode or for some other reason.

The plans for chapter 81 are not particularly detailed—there was no attempt to sketch the stages of the conversation or the form of the dialogue—but then no chapter in *Middlemarch* was planned in that manner; it was not George Eliot's way. But it *was* planned for. All the motives and events, for example, are in the notebook: that Dorothea has returned out of pity, that Rosamond is "wrought upon" by this pity or love, and that she tells Dorothea that it is Dorothea Will loves.

With this evidence of the preparation that went into the setting of this scene and of the number of entries mentioning this scene and revealing George Eliot's growing awareness of its subject and nature, it is difficult indeed to believe that although George Eliot " always knew they had, sooner or later, to come together, she kept the idea resolutely out of her mind until Dorothea was in Rosamond's drawing-room."

Certainly there is more evidence of "simmering" than there is of sudden "possession" in the planning of this scene, and the *Blackwood's* article seems closer to the true picture of George Eliot's creative method than her husband's version. But what about the element on which they seem to agree, that George Eliot's manuscript was, in Blackwood's words, free of "blur or erasure," or, as Cross puts it with specific reference to chapter 81 of *Middlemarch*, that George Eliot "abandoning herself to the inspiration of the moment, . . . wrote the whole scene exactly as it stands, *without alteration or erasure*, in an intense state of excitement and agitation [italics mine]"?

The clear sense of this passage is not only that there were no revisions in the manuscript of this chapter after this fit of inspiration—"exactly as it stands"—but that there were no changes even during the moment of inspiration—"without alteration or erasure."

It is not true. Indeed, this chapter was more heavily revised than were most of the others in *Middlemarch*. It would perhaps be useful to go through the chapter revision by revision indicating what changes were made in the manuscript, even though some of the deleted passages are no longer legible. Not only will this show us to what extent Cross's statement is untrue or misleading, but it will show us the nature and extent of the changes George Eliot made in manuscript. For if there are more changes in this chapter than there are in the average chapter in *Middlemarch*, they are not so much more numerous as to make the chapter atypical.

There are no revisions at all on the first manuscript page of chapter 81.[3] An unrevised page is so unusual in George Eliot's manuscript of *Middlemarch* that one is immediately inclined either to believe Cross's version of the inspired writing of this chapter or to suspect that the page had been rewritten. The last line of the page appears in the bottom margin, often a sign that George Eliot was rewriting a page and spacing it to meet an already completed one. The motto at the head of the

[3] Page ends 3: 396, " her into the drawing-room, he."

chapter clearly was added at a later time: unlike the rest of the page it is in violet ink and spaced two written lines to each ruled line.

With the end of page 91 the lack of revision ends. The next page [4] contains a number of individually rather minor changes. In the very first sentence, Lydgate's rather pompous " one "—" When one is grateful . . . one does not "—is changed to the regal " we " and changed back again. In the next paragraph, " suddenly doubting " has been substituted for " checked by [word illegible] doubt " because " cheque " appears in the next sentence: " ' Yes, the cheque is going to Bulstrode today.' " Similar revisions toward the end of the page avoid repetition of " surprise." There are a number of other minor changes on this page, as there are throughout the chapter, which shall not be discussed for lack of space. On page 92, however, one change at least is substantial: " He [Lydgate] had told her of Dorothea's letter containing the cheque, and afterwards " has been inserted in the manuscript, so that in the new version Rosamond is prepared for her confession by being immediately put consciously in Dorothea's debt. Preparation for Rosamond's confession accounts for other relatively important changes. We first see Rosamond in this chapter as she

sat languidly considering what she should do next, her natural industry in small things always [5] prompting her to begin some kind of occupation . . .	sat languidly wondering what she should do next, her habitual industry in small things, even in the days of her sadness, prompting her to begin some kind of occupation . . .[6]

The addition of " wondering " and " sadness " has a small but appreciable effect in turning our sympathies toward Rosamond, up to now— with all her selfish " considering "—an object of our blame and hatred. The minor shift from " natural " to " habitual " keeps the point of view less than omniscient, keeps it outside Rosamond at this point; manipulation of point of view was an important factor in George Eliot's revision of this chapter.

The first half of page 93 has almost no revisions, and the rest of the page contains only minor ones. A change in one sentence of Rosamond's dialogue [7] perhaps tones down her imperiousness, and a later change rephrases an awkwardly quoted thought, making it indirect and eliminating repetition of forms of " trust."

[4] Page ends 3: 397, " she coloured and gave rather a."

[5] " Always " was first replaced by " still," then by the phrase in the right-hand column.

[6] The original version is on the left, the revised version on the right, here and throughout this chapter.

[7] From, " ' Tell Martha not to let any one else into the drawing-room,' " to " ' Pray tell Martha not to bring any one else ' " etc.

There are two beginnings for manuscript page 94. The first, clearly numbered " 94," is a fifty-word passage on the back of the last manuscript page of chapter 81 (p. 112) :

sibility. Will had wounded her too sharply for her to feel any compunction towards him & Dorothea: she felt her own injury too keenly to feel theirs, & in the hour of her bruised pride she had been compelled to feel that her much offending husband was after all her best refuge.

The last four syllables of " impossibility " which begin the earlier version of this page George Eliot inserted in the bottom margin of page 93; she thus began the new page 94 with " Will." Besides eliminating " the hour of her bruised pride " and the repetitions of " feel," the new version represents a change in tactics: though we are at this point to sympathize with Rosamond to some extent, as the changes on page 92 indicate, and though in this chapter she is partially to atone for her sins, the shift from the hateful to the sympathetic Rosamond cannot be made too quickly—Rosamond must act with uncharacteristic selflessness only under the impact of Dorothea's own selflessness. This same consideration is perhaps responsible for many of the other revisions which stud the remainder of page 94:

Dorothea was not only the " preferred " woman, but had also a formidable hold on Rosamond as a benefactor of her husband; [to] poor Rosamond's pained confused vision it seemed that this Mrs. Casaubon—this woman who predominated in all things concerning her—must have come to her with the sense of her advantage, and with an animosity that must make her desire to use it. Indeed, not Rosamond only, but any one else, knowing only the outer facts of the case, and not the simple inspiration on which Dorothea acted, might well have wondered what she came for.

Looking likely [sic] the lovely ghost of herself, her graceful slimness wrapped in her soft white shawl, the rounded infant-like lips inevitably mild and innocent, Rosamond paused at three yards' distance from her visitor and bowed. But Dorothea, who had taken off her gloves, from an impulse which she could never resist when she wanted a sense of freedom, and looking with

Dorothea was not only the " preferred " woman, but had also a formidable advantage in being Lydgate's benefactor; and to poor Rosamond's pained confused vision it seemed that this Mrs. Casaubon—this woman who predominated in all things concerning her—must have come now with the sense of having the advantage, and with animosity prompting her to use it. Indeed, not Rosamond only, but any one else, knowing the outer facts of the case, and not the simple inspiration on which Dorothea acted, might well have wondered why she came.

Looking like the lovely ghost of herself, her graceful slimness wrapped in her soft white shawl, the rounded infantine mouth and cheek inevitably suggesting mildness and innocence, Rosamond paused at three yards' distance from her visitor and bowed. But Dorothea, who had taken off her gloves, from an impulse which she could never resist when she wanted a open sadness into Rosamond's [8] put out her hand. Rosamond could not avoid meeting her glance, could not avoid putting her little hand into Dorothea's, which clasped it with gentle motherliness; and immediately a doubt of her own prepossessions began to stir within her. Rosamond's eye was quick for faces; she saw Dorothea's face looked pale and changed since yesterday, yet gentle.

sense of freedom, came forward, and with her face full of a sad yet sweet openness, put out her hand. Rosamond could not avoid meeting her glance, could not avoid putting her small hand into Dorothea's, which clasped it with gentle motherliness; and immediately a doubt of her own prepossessions began to stir within her. Rosamond's eye was quick for faces; she saw Mrs. Casaubon's face looked pale and changed since yesterday, yet gentle (3: 398-99).

Related to the timing of Rosamond's confession is the delicate manipulation of point of view highlighted by the revision of this page. An important element in this chapter is the misunderstanding of each woman about the other: Rosamond thinks Dorothea has come to upbraid her or to gloat; Dorothea believes Will loves Rosamond. The omniscient reader knows all, but it is essential that he understand the feelings caused by each woman's limited knowledge of the other; the point of view thus shifts delicately from one of the women to the other and between internal and external views of them and of the situation. Up to the last sentence of the first paragraph on the page, events are seen through Rosamond's mind. There is a shift to an external viewer—" any one else "—but with an appeal to the omniscience of the reader: we know " the simple inspiration on which Dorothea acted." The beginning of the second paragraph maintains this external view—of what Rosamond looks like—though this may be seen through Dorothea's eyes, and the same ambivalent point of view is maintained through the explanation of Dorothea's impulse to remove her gloves; the view then moves outside Dorothea—to see Dorothea's look—on its way back to Rosamond: Rosamond " could not avoid," " a doubt . . . began to stir within her." Many of the revisions here, as in other passages in this chapter, may be attributed to these subtle shifts: e. g., the change from " mild and innocent " to the carefully external " suggesting mildness and innocence " [9] and the change from the too friendly and familiar " Dorothea's face " to " Mrs. Casaubon's face " which keeps the point of view Rosamond's.

The next manuscript page, 95, contains very few revisions, and most

[8] The incomplete structure in this version apparently indicates that George Eliot made the revision in mid-sentence. Where this seems to be the case in passages quoted below, no notation will be made.

[9] George Eliot apparently made this change in proof, since the manuscript reads like the original. Bound proof of the first edition corrected by the author is in the possession of Wing Commander G. D. Blackwood, who very kindly permitted me to examine it, but proof of this chapter is missing.

of these were made either during the writing of the sentence in which they appear or in proof. The last word of the page, "deal," [10] is in the bottom margin, perhaps an indication that this page was rewritten from an earlier version, though there is no other concrete evidence to this effect.

Page 96 [11] contains few revisions, but some of these are rather extensive,[12] and one reveals a shift in tactics:

Of course Mrs. Casaubon had the facts in her mind—she had been suffering—she loved [word illegible] Will [word illegible] words implied ⟨he knew⟩ [13] it.	Of course Mrs. Casaubon had the facts in her mind, but she was not going to speak of anything connected with them.

The deleted passage dealt too directly with the Will-Dorothea situation, which George Eliot wanted to keep at this point as an undercurrent, not as a force on the surface of the action, so that Dorothea may not seem to be seeking a favor in exchange for her kindness and may not seem even to suspect that Rosamond has anything to tell her about Will. Both these changes, however, involve incomplete original passages, George Eliot making them while writing the very sentence in which they appear.

The first part of page 97,[14] like the two pages preceding it, is relatively unrevised; Dorothea's speech, which makes up half the page, contains only a few minor changes. Revision of the next paragraph, however, is rather interesting:

Dorothea's face had become animated, and as it beamed on Rosamond very close to her, she felt something like ⟨awe⟩ of a ⟨supernatural⟩ presence at this self-forgetful ardour in look and speech. Blushing she said, with embarrassment, "Thank you: you are very kind."	Dorothea's face had become animated, and as it beamed on Rosamond very close to her, she felt something like bashful timidity before a superior, in the presence of this self-forgetful ardour. She said with blushing embarrassment, "Thank you: you are very kind."

If this reading of the almost illegible deleted passage is correct, the gist of the revision is clear: it tones down somewhat the already embarrassing adulation of Dorothea by the other characters in the novel (and by the author), and, insofar as it does, it improves the passage for those who find George Eliot's praise of her heroine excessive.

[10] Page ends 3: 399, "to know a great deal."

[11] Page ends 3: 400, "He confessed to me."

[12] For example, the change from "The cordial, pleading tones which seemed in this warm flow to be utterly heedless of," to, "The cordial, pleading tones which seemed to flow with generous heedlessness."

[13] Pointed brackets enclose conjectural reading of partially legible words in the manuscript.

[14] Page ends 3: 401, "that his misfortunes must."

Extensive revision begins again about the middle of page 98. The opening paragraphs contain revisions only on the order of those on pages 95-97, but the paragraph which ends the page was significantly altered:

Rosamond felt her inward wound pang, as if a wound had been pierced, burst into crying as she had done the day before, and clung to Dorothea's arm ⟨and must have⟩ [at least one word illegible] her husband's. Poor Dorothea was feeling a great wave of her sorrow returning over her as her thought was [word illegible] drawn to the possible share that Will Ladislaw might have in ⟨any⟩ Rosamond's mental tumult. She was beginning to fear that she should not be able to suppress herself enough to the end of this meeting, and while Rosamond was clinging to her, she was struggling against her own sobs.

Rosamond, with an over-mastering pang, as if a wound within her had been probed, burst into hysterical crying as she had done the day before when she clung to her husband. Poor Dorothea was feeling a great wave of her own sorrow returning over her— her thought being drawn to the possible share that Will Ladislaw might have in Rosamond's mental tumult. She was beginning to fear that she should not be able to suppress herself enough to the end of this meeting, and while her hand was still resting on Rosamond's lap, though the hand underneath it was withdrawn, she was struggling against her own rising sobs (3: 402).

Though Rosamond is crying, even hysterical, she is not yet ready to reach out for Dorothea, to cling to her. Rosamond, like her hand, is as yet withdrawn.

Neither the paragraph nor the changes end with the end of page 98; page 99 [15] begins:

She tried to master herself with the thought that this might be the turning-point in three lives—not her own; no, there the irrevocable had happened, but—in the lives of those three lives which were touching hers with the solemn neighbourhood of danger and distress. The fragile creature who was crying close to her—there might still be time to bring her back into the ⟨confidence and faithfulness from⟩ which she was ⟨wandering⟩ was unlike any other: she and Rosamond could never be together again with the same thrilling consciousness of yesterday within them both.

She tried to master herself with the thought that this might be the turning-point in three lives—not her own; no, there the irrevocable had happened, but—in those three lives which were touching hers with the solemn neighbourhood of danger and distress. The fragile creature who was crying close to her—there might still be time to rescue her from the misery of false incompatible bonds; and this moment was unlike any other: she and Rosamond could never be together again with the same thrilling consciousness of yesterday within them both. She felt the relation between them to be peculiar enough to give her a peculiar influence, though she had no conception that the way in which her own feelings were involved was fully known to Mrs. Lydgate.

[15] Page ends 3: 403, " Pride was broken down between these two."

The purpose of lessening Rosamond's "offense" at this point is not clear; to "bring back" suggests an error already committed, to "rescue" one which can still be avoided; escape from "false incompatible bonds" is certainly more abstract and possibly less severe than a breach of "confidence and faithfulness." Perhaps it was to make Rosamond's atonement more conceivable, some preparation for it being necessary; perhaps it was to reveal, since this is a statement of what was in Dorothea's mind, that Dorothea, despite her better judgment, was still unwilling to believe what she thought she had seen the day before, and that she was hoping for an outcome like that which was indeed forthcoming. The long sentence which concludes this paragraph was written on the back of the page with a note to "Insert" and on the front a note to "See Back," a form of revision rare in George Eliot's manuscript. The sentence serves as a transition between Dorothea's point of view, which has dominated the paragraph from "Poor Dorothea" (p. 98) and Rosamond's point of view, which dominates the next paragraph. It also helps explain why Dorothea feels free to go on with her advice: by specifying that Dorothea is ignorant of Rosamond's knowledge of the emotional relationship between Will and Dorothea, George Eliot makes her continuing both more credible and less hypocritical, for if Dorothea were aware that Rosamond knew of that relationship, her continuing would have been a conscious playing on the affections of Rosamond. That Dorothea is not doing so even now is hard to believe.

That neither woman truly understands the full extent either of the emotions or of the knowledge of the other is underlined once again in the next paragraph by the only other significant revisions on the page; George Eliot is describing Rosamond's reaction:

this strange unexpected manifestation of feeling in Dorothea a woman whom she had approached with a shrinking aversion and dread made her soul totter . . .	this strange unexpected manifestation of feeling in a woman whom she had approached with a shrinking aversion and dread, as one who must necessarily have a jealous hatred towards her, made her soul totter. . . .

The deletion of "Dorothea" emphasizes that Rosamond and Dorothea are still more or less strangers, and the added phrase emphasizes Rosamond's misunderstanding of what was going on in Dorothea's soul, Rosamond judging Dorothea by her own, or at least by human, standards.

George Eliot apparently rewrote completely some of the pages between 100 and 104: she changed page numbers and wrote words in the bottom margin. Exactly which pages she rewrote cannot be ascertained, but the three pages now numbered 100-102 seem to be second drafts of two earlier pages, 100-101. Since some of these pages, particularly the early ones, seem to have been rewritten, they naturally now contain but few re-visions, and these are minor. But from the end of the first full paragraph on page 102 through Rosamond's confession of what had actually taken place between her and Will the day before—in some ways the heart of the chapter—there were frequent, extensive, and significant revisions, particularly in the description of how Rosamond speaks while confessing:

" You are thinking what is not true," said Rosamond while she was still feeling Dorothea's arms round her—a necessity to free herself from something that oppressed her as if it were blood-guiltiness.

They moved apart, looking at each other.
" When you came in yesterday—it was not as you thought," said Rosa-mond ⟨in a low tone⟩.
There was a movement of surprised attention in Dorothea [word illegible]. She expected a vindication of Rosa-mond herself.
" He was telling me he loved another woman, ⟨and⟩ that I might know he could never love me. And now I think he hates me because—because you mistook him yesterday. He says it is through me that you will think ill of him—think that he is a false person. But it shall not be through me ⟨which⟩ [several words illegible] ⟨bitterness⟩,"—Rosamond now spoke with her utmost distinctness and deter-mination. . . .

" You are thinking what is not true," said Rosamond, in an eager half-whisper, while she was still feeling Dorothea's arms round her—urged by a mysterious necessity to free herself from something that oppressed her as if it were blood-guiltiness.

They moved apart, looking at each other.
" When you came in yesterday—it was not as you thought," said Rosa-mond in the same tone.
There was a movement of surprised attention in Dorothea. She expected a vindication of Rosamond herself.
" He was telling me he loved an-other woman, that I might know he could never love me," said Rosamond, getting more and more hurried as she went on. " And now I think he hates me because—because you mistook him yesterday. He says it is through me that you will think ill of him—think that he is a false person. But it shall not be through me " (3: 406) .

What these revisions of stage directions constitute is not only a change in the tone of the passage but a deeper insight, or the presentation of that insight, into how a Rosamond would feel, speak, and act at this juncture. A scene in which the villain repents and thereby insures the happiness of the hero and heroine is difficult to justify in any work demanding more *vraisemblance* than comedy. This scene requires just such a switch in the actions of a character hitherto presented as shallow, vain, and egocentric, incapable of imagining the feelings of others. How can George Eliot motivate such a change? How can she present it? The motivation she points out in the paragraph following the confession:

Rosamond had delivered her soul under impulses which she had not known before. She had begun her confession under the subduing influence of Dorothea's emotion; and as she went on she had gathered the sense that she was repelling Will's reproaches, which were still like a knife-wound within her.

In the original version of this scene, Rosamond, with Dorothea's arms around her, feels that it is necessary to confess, and when the women move apart, Rosamond's voice becomes more distinct and she becomes conscious of confessing, determined to go on. In the revised version, with the addition of the " eager half-whisper " and "mysterious " urge, the unconscious element of Rosamond's beginning to confess—she is under the influence of a stronger, deeper-feeling personality—is emphasized, and when the two women move apart Rosamond speaks not more determinedly, but more hastily; her confession was triggered by Dorothea's arms about her, by Dorothea's emotion, but, once she began, the memory of Will's accusations of the day before gave impetus to the confession and kept it pouring forth. The revisions, in other words, underline the unconsciousness of the impulse which makes Rosamond begin to tell the truth and motivates the latter part of the unburdening, still unconscious, by the remembered experience of Will's galling speech of the day before, which Rosamond, whose very vanity would cause her to store up this speech, has had festering within her. The revisions thus make the action justify the author's analysis which follows; that analysis perhaps caused the revision, George Eliot herself only growing aware of the motivation as she wrote it.

Revision of this delicately balanced confession scene continues at the bottom of page 102 [16] and at the top of page 103,[17] not, as before, in the description of Rosamond's tone, but in the substance of what she actually says:

". . . He has never had any love for me. He has always thought slightly of me. I imagined that he had some regard for me, but now I am sure that [18] he had none. He said yesterday that no other woman existed for him beside you. The blame of what happened is entirely mine. He said he could never explain to you—he is in despair. He said he would not sacrifice me—[about two words illegible] by telling you that I had shown my feeling too strongly. He is in despair because

". . . He has never had any love for me—I know he has not—he has always thought slightly of me. He said yesterday that no other woman existed for him beside you. The blame of what happened is entirely mine. He said he could never explain to you—because of me. He said you could never think well of him again. But now I have told you, and he cannot reproach me any more."

[16] Page ends 3: 406, " slightly of me. He said."
[17] Page ends 3: 407, " I was very unhappy. I am." For facsimile of this manuscript page, see Illustration 4, Appendix A.
[18] The phrase " now I am sure that " was inserted before the entire passage was deleted.

you will never think well of him again.
But now I have told you, you will and
he cannot reproach me any more."

The revised version does not merely gain in economy, but again, consciously or unconsciously, thoroughly realizes the character of Rosamond:
even under the mysterious impulse, even with the promptings of a guilt
feeling and the desire, based on her vanity, to negate the words Will
flung at her the day before, even then, some of Rosamond's vanity and
self-righteousness assert themselves—the revision eliminates three uses of
" I " in a blameworthy connection prior to the last self-congratulatory
sentence and substitutes just one; it eliminates from her confession the
facts that she imagined Will loved her and that she revealed her feelings
about him. Rosamond still shoulders the blame, but what she is guilty
of is stated in abstract terms, and in terms of Will's reaction (which
caused this part of the confession in the first place) rather than in terms
of her own actions or thoughts. Thus, even while rising far enough out
of character to confess, Rosamond, in the revised passage, preserves
enough of her own character to make the confession credible.

Other revisions on page 103 deal chiefly with Dorothea's reaction to
Rosamond's confession:

she could only feel that this would be joy when she had recovered her power of feeling it. But she immediately [one or two words illegible] response to Rosamond's last words and said earnestly,	she could only perceive that this would be joy when she had recovered her power of feeling it. Her immediate consciousness was one of immense sympathy without check; she cared for Rosamond without struggle now, and responded earnestly to her last words—
"No, he cannot reproach you any more."	"No, he cannot reproach you any more."
	With her usual tendency to over-estimate the good in others, she felt a great outgoing of her heart towards Rosamond, for the generous effort which had redeemed her from suffer-ing, not counting that the effort was a reflex of her own energy.[19]

The sentence added to the first of these paragraphs reminds the reader
that Dorothea's struggle with jealousy had not been finally won at dawn
but has been continuing throughout her visit; up to this point she has
been able to care for Rosamond only by force of will. Even though the

[19] It is difficult to tell what, if any, of this paragraph was in the first version of this
page. From "With" to "great" may have been added in the space left by para-
graphing—it begins immediately after "more" with no new paragraph indicated;
"her from suffering, not count—" was added in the left margin of the manuscript
page.

extent of the revision of the last paragraph is not certain, its purpose seems clear: it gives almost all the credit for Rosamond's confession to Dorothea. If this change does help explain Rosamond's uncharacteristic generosity, it makes Dorothea's goodness almost unbearable—not all changes are improvements.

Revisions on page 104 [20] and up to the last paragraph on page 105, the last paragraph of the chapter, are numerous but of relatively minor importance. Changes in the last paragraph, however, significantly alter the ending of the chapter; Rosamond is speaking to Lydgate after Dorothea has left:

"I think she has," said Rosamond. "She told me that you said you would not do anything stay in Middlemarch [21] or do anything that I disliked."	"I think she has," said **Rosamond,** looking up in his face.

The original version of the chapter ends here, but George Eliot, after revising the first sentence, wrote, apparently in several stages, a new ending:

"How heavy your eyes are, Tertius—and do push your hair back." He lifted his large white hand to obey her, and felt thankful for this little mark of interest in him. Poor Rosamond's vagrant fancy had come back terribly scourged [22]—meek enough to nestle under the old despised shelter. And the shelter was still there: Lydgate had accepted his [23] narrowed lot with sad resignation. He had chosen this fragile creature, and had taken the burthen of her life upon his arms. He must walk as he could, carrying that burthen pitifully.

George Eliot wrote the first two sentences in the bottom margin and the rest of the passage on the back of the page. She wrote the inserted passage from "Poor Rosamond's" on the back of the page, and from "meek" on wrote the passage in violet ink, adding it, apparently, at a later date, perhaps when she was rereading this portion of the novel before sending it off to the publisher (see description of the manuscript below, p. 133 in "Bibliography").

Chapter 81 thus was originally to have ended, "'She told me that you said you would not do anything . . . that I disliked,'" with the galling reassertion of Rosamond's vanity and egocentric single-mindedness, the interview with Dorothea and her experience of the day before having

[20] Page ends 3: 408, "'order your carriage to come for you?'"

[21] George Eliot inserted "stay in Middlemarch" and perhaps deleted the first "do anything" before deleting the entire passage.

[22] Deleted here in mid-sentence was, "its bruised hope [word illegible] glad enough to nestle under."

[23] The phrase "accepted his" was substituted for "endured with sad resignation," apparently in mid-sentence.

had no lasting effect on her at all. But this reversion to type was too swift and too complete. Rosamond could not be expected to change completely, but she had for the first time been compelled to look at life from a point of view not her own, and this experience must be allowed some influence, no matter how slight. In the bottom margin and on the back of the page George Eliot devised a new ending: Rosamond has been affected by her experiences with Will and Dorothea; she has been forced to return to her husband's protection and in some measure to appreciate it. But she still is Rosamond enough to make even her tenderness a form of domination—" '. . . do push your hair back.' " George Eliot also added Lydgate's reaction: his resignation, his shortening of the lines of his existence. This, too, changes the tone. Had George Eliot not revised, the chapter would have ended on a note of shrill hatred for Rosamond and of disgust with Lydgate for not asserting himself once and for all. It now ends quite differently, on a note of pity for both Lydgates, almost like that pity we felt earlier in the novel (chapter 74) for the Bulstrodes when Harriet stood beside her husband, as Lydgate, in a somewhat similar gesture, now stands beside his wife.

That George Eliot was inspired when she wrote chapter 81 of *Middlemarch* may well be true, but that " she kept the idea " of this chapter " resolutely out of her mind until Dorothea was in Rosamond's drawing-room " is contradicted by her notebook, and that " she wrote the whole scene exactly as it stands, without alteration or erasure " is contradicted by the manuscript of the novel.

George Eliot's Quarry for " Middlemarch " reveals that she considered several possible occasions for the scene, that she concerned herself in advance with defining Dorothea's motive in coming to see Rosamond and Rosamond's in confessing, and that she had the main ideas of the chapter in mind before she began writing it.

The manuscript reveals that the author made some changes while writing, others later when she was reading the manuscript over, and still others when reading proof. She changed a word, a phrase, a sentence, or a passage. She added passages on the backs of pages. She rewrote whole pages, groups of consecutive pages. She made changes in every stage of writing and of almost every possible extent.

She made changes in matters of style and changes in the matter itself. Chief among the latter were those made necessary by the need for careful timing, presentation, and motivation of Rosamond's out-of-character speech. George Eliot had also to manipulate the point of view very carefully and subtly, shifting it delicately back and forth between the two women, a manipulation which necessitated careful revision. Finally, she revised the tone of the end of the chapter, changing Rosamond's too quick and total reversion to hateful type to show her scarred, if still selfish, together with her husband an object of pity as well as blame.

So this chapter, which, according to Cross, George Eliot herself identified as having been written spontaneously and without change, was, in fact, prepared for with reasonable care and was revised in all stages of its evolution and in almost all its aspects: timing, content, point of view, characterization, tone, and outcome. Writing, to George Eliot, was not an unpremeditated outpouring; neither was it a mechanical following of detailed blueprint. It was a process of evolution and of discovery.

The beginning of *Middlemarch* flowed together from its twin sources in the earlier "Middlemarch" and "Miss Brooke." The amount of plot material on hand after this joining required more space than the conventional three-decker could afford, and to suit this need Lewes originated the half-volume parts form, which form in turn made demands upon the novel and dictated certain changes in its nature. When the novel was well under way but progress was still uncertain, George Eliot paused to sketch out plans for the last five parts in her notebook, and she continued to use the notebook to outline portions of the novel, block off parts, study relationships of one plot line to the other, and otherwise prepare the scaffolding for the last portion of the novel. She was not a slave to her own plans, however; she changed them even as she wrote when new relationships and developments impossible to anticipate revealed themselves. And throughout this process, throughout the writing of the novel—even in chapter 81 but not peculiarly or particularly in that chapter—she made changes. These revisions, both of plan and of the words already written, which George Eliot made while writing and even after writing, give a depth and richness to the novel which no mechanical adherence to outline could have done. In this writing process such terms as "spontaneous" and "contrived," "conscious" or "unconcious" have no meaning. The whole being, the artist, struggles with his medium, words, and through them both expresses and discovers what he has to say. What, in 1869-72, George Eliot had to say is *Middlemarch*.

Appendix A

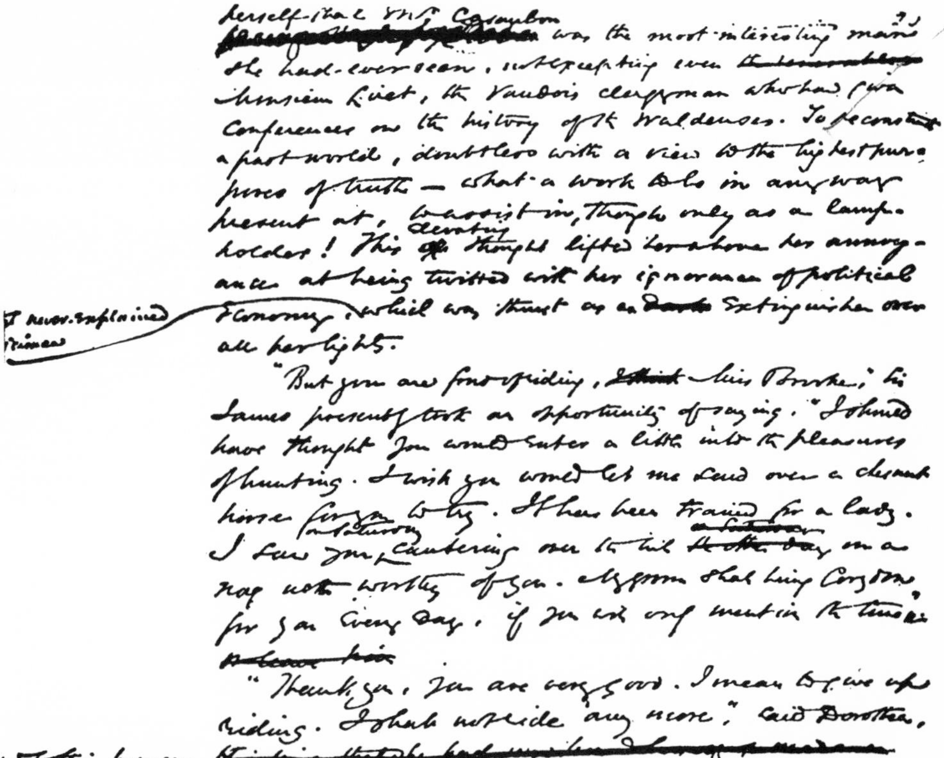

Illustration 1. B.M. Add. MSS. 34,034, Cabinet Edition 1: 23, chapter 2. A typical page from "Miss Brooke" on Parkins and Gotto unlined paper probably written before it was joined to "Middlemarch." See above, p. 5, *et seq.*

[Manuscript page of heavily revised handwritten text by George Eliot, with numerous crossings-out and marginal insertions. The body is a draft passage concerning Lydgate's childhood and education. Marginal notes include "three," "practising doctors / city practitioners," "then," "already," and "after a conversation of Lydgate and appearance..."]

Illustration 2. B.M. Add. MSS. 34,034, Cabinet Edition 1: 215, chapter 15. A semipaced page on " 1869 " ruled paper probably rewritten when " Miss Brooke " was being joined to " Middlemarch " and based on original introduction to " Middlemarch." This page, numbered 161 by George Eliot, is quite heavily revised and includes one revision of Lydgate's first name from " Tristram " to " Tertius " (l. 9). See above, page 24. It is largely through the semispacing of certain manuscript pages such as this one that George Eliot's fusion of " Middlemarch " and " Miss Brooke " can be traced. See above, pp. 19-36.

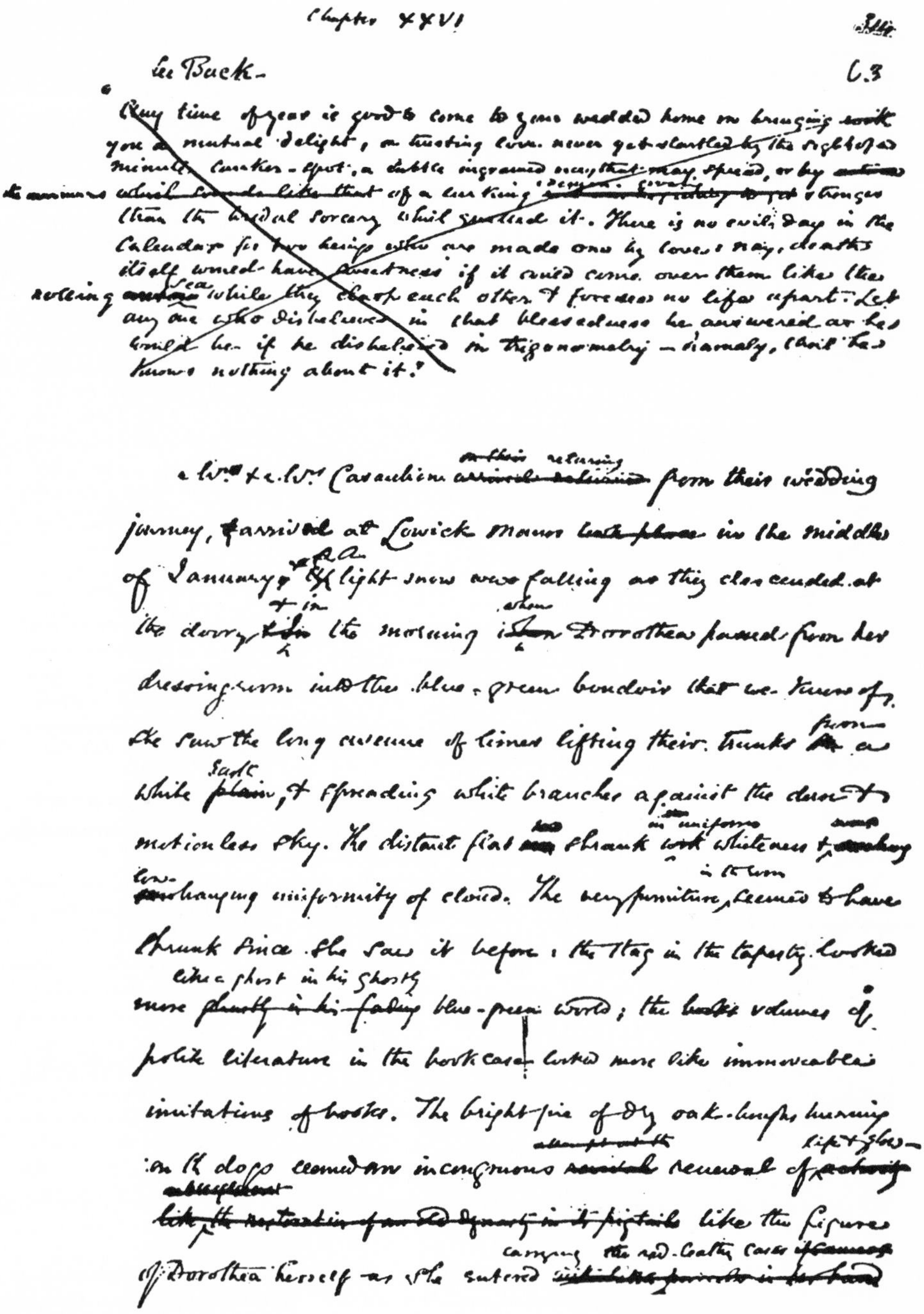
Chapter XXVI

See Buck- C.3

Any time of year is good to come to your wedded home on bringing you a mutual delight, or trusting love never yet startled by the sight of a minute canker-spot, a dabble ingrained way that may spread, or by omens which sound like that of a creeping [illegible] stronger than the bridal sorcery which greeted it. There is no evil day in the Calendar for two beings who are made one by love: nay, death itself would have sweetness if it could come over them like the rolling sea while they clasp each other & foresee no life apart. Let any one who disbelieves in that blessedness be answered as he would be if he disbelieved in trigonometry — namely, that he knows nothing about it.

Mr. & Mrs. Casaubon, returning from their wedding journey, arrived at Lowick Manor in the middle of January. A light snow was falling as they descended at the door, & in the morning when Dorothea passed from her dressing-room into the blue-green boudoir that we know of, she saw the long avenue of limes lifting their trunks from a white earth, & spreading white branches against the dun & motionless sky. The distant flat shrank in uniform whiteness & low-hanging uniformity of cloud. The very furniture in the room seemed to have shrunk since she saw it before: the stag in the tapestry looked more like a ghost in his ghostly blue-green world; the volumes of polite literature in the bookcase looked more like immoveable imitations of books. The bright fire of dry oak-boughs burning on the dogs seemed an incongruous renewal of life & glow — like the figure of Dorothea herself as she entered carrying the red-leather cases

Illustration 3. B.M. Add. MSS. 34,035, p. 63, Cabinet Edition 2: [1], the opening page of chapter 28. Notice the chapter is still numbered "xxvi"; it was to have followed the Dorothea in Rome chapters (now 19-22 but at one time 22-24, then 22-25). The deleted number "314" (chapter 22 ends with manuscript page 313 in that sequence) also reveals this shift. See above, p. 53. Otherwise this page, on "1869" paper and regularly spaced, is rather typical of the *Middlemarch* manuscript in appearance and number and extent of revisions; even deletion of motto is common in manuscript.

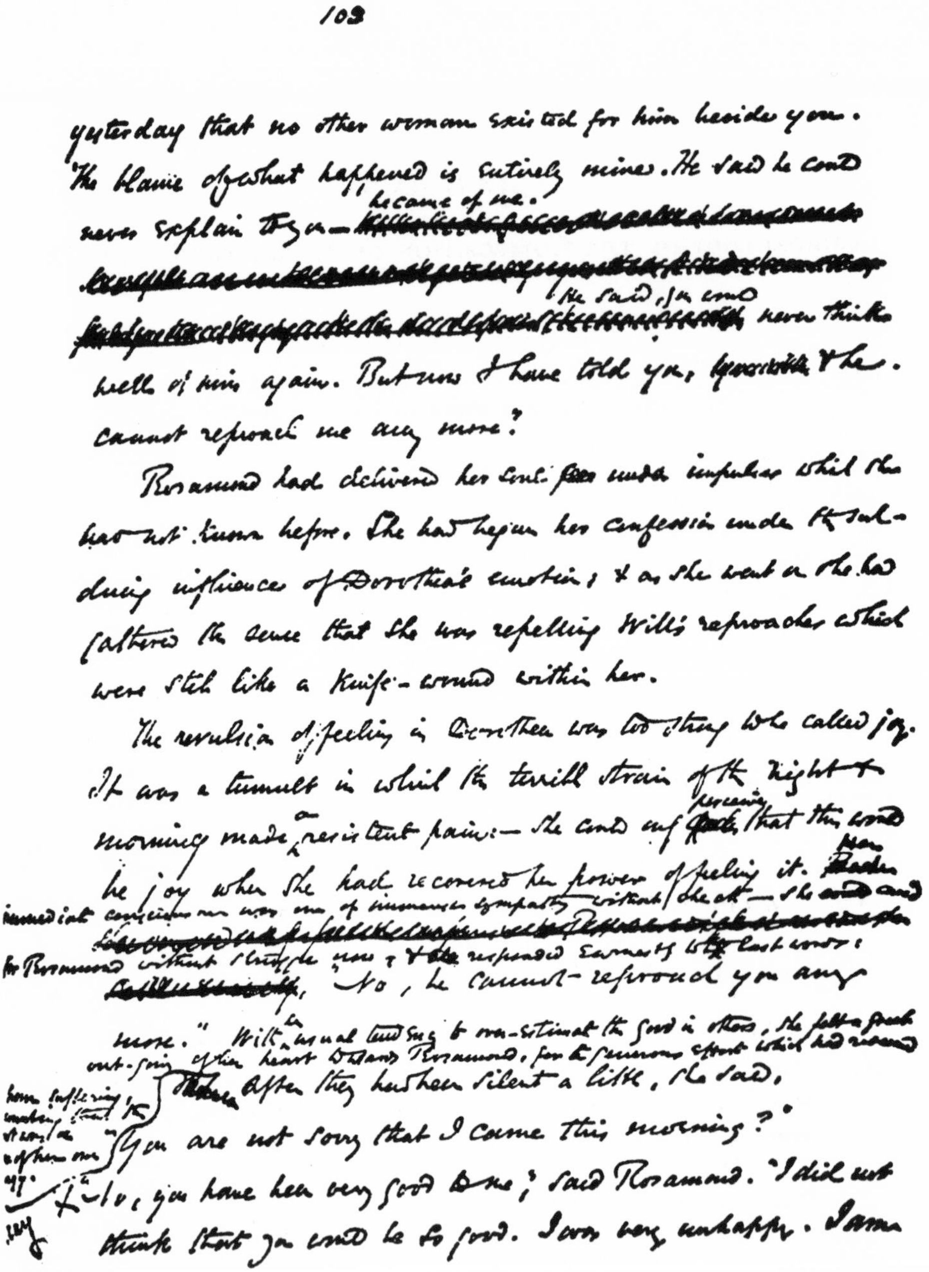
103

yesterday that no other woman existed for him beside you. The blame of what happened is entirely mine. He said he could never explain to you—because of me. He said you could never think well of him again. But now I have told you, & he cannot reproach me any more?

Rosamond had delivered her confession under impulses which she had not known before. She had begun her confession under the subduing influence of Dorothea's emotion; & as she went on she had gathered the sense that she was repelling Will's reproaches which were still like a knife-wound within her.

The revulsion of feeling in Dorothea was too strong to be called joy. It was a tumult in which the terrible strain of the night & morning made a resistant pain:—she could only perceive that this would be joy when she had recovered her power of feeling it. Her immediate consciousness was one of immense sympathy without check—she cared for Rosamond without struggle now, & she responded earnestly to her last words: "No, he cannot reproach you any more." With her usual tendency to over-estimate the good in others, she felt a great out-going of her heart towards Rosamond, for the generous effort which had redeemed her from suffering, not counting that the effort was a reflex of her own energy. After they had been silent a little, she said,

"You are not sorry that I came this morning?"

"No, you have been very good to me," said Rosamond. "I did not think that you could be so good. I was very unhappy. I am

Illustration 4. B.M. Add. MSS. 34,037, Cabinet Edition 3: 406-7, chapter 81. A page from the chapter George Eliot told her husband she wrote without alteration or erasure. The "103" is the author's page number in her Book 8 series. This page contains the last part of Rosamond's confession to Dorothea that Rosamond and not Will Ladislaw was responsible for the emotional scene Dorothea witnessed the day before. See above, pp. 119-21. Revisions on this page, typical of those throughout the chapter, contradict hitherto accepted descriptions of George Eliot's creative method.

Appendix B

CHRONOLOGY OF THE COMPOSITION OF *Middlemarch*, 1867-72

I. PROJECTED UNNAMED WORKS

1867	March	16	Projected construction of two prose works.
		21	" Private projects about an English novel."

II. " MIDDLEMARCH "

1869	Jan.	1	Projected novel called " Middlemarch."
		23	A little progress in construction.
	Feb.	19	Plan already sketched; elements in mind for years.
	July	19	" Writing an introduction to ' Middlemarch.' "
	Aug.	2	Began " Middlemarch."
		5	Finished chapter 1.
	Sept.	1	Up to beginning of chapter 3.
		11	Finished chapter 3, 50 pp.
		21	Requests information about hospitals.
1870	March	7	Novel creeps on.
		20	Novel languishing.

III. " MISS BROOKE "

1870	Nov.	early	Starts " Miss Brooke " as separate story.
	Dec.	2	At p. 44 [end of chapter 4].
	Dec.	31	Finished 100 pp. [middle of chapter 10].

IV. COMPOSITION AND PARTS PUBLICATION OF *Middlemarch*

1871	March	19	Finished 236 pp. of [*Middlemarch*, chapters 1-18 and 23].
	May	7	Needs 4 vols. Lewes proposes parts publication.
	June	27	Finished Books 1 & 2.
	Oct.	29	Book 3 ready to set in type.
	Dec.	1	Book 1 published; 4 not finished.
		20	Writing chapter 37, working on construction.
1872	Jan.	18	Finished Book 4 (through chapter 41).
		29	Finished Book 4 including chapter 42.
	Feb.	1	Book 2 published.
	April		Book 3 published.
	May	8	Finished Book 5.
	June		Book 4 published.

July   2   Finished and mailed Book 6.
        13   Lewes proposes last three parts be published at monthly
             rather than bimonthly intervals.
July   29   Book 5 published.
Aug.   Reads Lewes chapters of Book 7.
        4   Book 7 mailed; " unfortunately delayed."
Sept.   2   90 pp. of Book 8, through chapter 80, mailed.
        9   30 more pages of Book 8 mailed [near end of chapter 83].
        11   [18 more pages] mailed; through chapter 84.
        13   Rest of Book 8, excluding " Finale " mailed.
Oct.   Book 6 published.
        2   " Finale " mailed.
Nov.   Book 7 published.
Dec.   Book 8 published.

Bibliography

I. Descriptions of Primary Sources

Eliot, George. *Middlemarch.* British Museum Additional Manuscripts 34,034–34,037. Four volumes, leather-bound, each volume containing two Books of *Middlemarch* and 291, 302, 313, and 311 manuscript pages respectively, according to a series of page numbers in pencil presumably added by the British Museum or the binder. George Eliot numbered pages in ink, frequently changing them—resulting occasionally in two or even three numbers on the page and such addenda as " 130a," etc.; through the first two volumes she numbered consecutively within the volume, afterwards by the part or half-volume. She wrote on one side of the page only (except for rare addenda, chiefly mottoes, on the backs of pages) and used a very dark brown, almost black ink, changing some time in 1872 to a violet ink in which she wrote many changes and some pages in the last part of the novel. Paper stocks vary, though each measured approximately seven by nine inches before trimming (as much as a quarter-inch lost in the process). The first part of the manuscript (1: 3-116 and 1: 175-76) is on Parkins and Gotto watermarked, unlined paper. The rest of the manuscript is on paper with 23 blue ruled lines to the page. In the first and second volumes and in scattered pages throughout the rest of the manuscript the lined paper is watermarked " T & [J]H 1869 "; in the third volume it is watermarked with the same initials and, chiefly, " 1870," with scattered pages containing those initials and " Kent "; in the fourth volume chiefly " Kent " appears with some " 1870 " and even some " 1869 " pages scattered through. Throughout most of the manuscript George Eliot wrote only on the ruled lines, but in 1: 135-44 (139 is the title page of Book 2) and 1: 165-74, she semispaced, i. e., wrote one line on and one line between each ruled line, or about 45 lines per page.

Kitchel, Anna Theresa (ed.). *George Eliot's Quarry for " Middlemarch."* Berkeley and Los Angeles: University of California Press, 1950.

After telling how Amy Lowell bought the *Quarry* from Quaritch and left it to Harvard University upon her death in 1925, Miss Kitchel (p. 1) describes the notebook as

a small, black leather notebook, $4\frac{1}{8}$ by $6\frac{1}{2}$ in. On the cover an undecipherable title in gilt script is concealed by a paper label inscribed in George Eliot's hand, " Quarry for Middlemarch." About half the book is devoted principally to notes on scientific, and especially medical, matters, with three pages, 23, 24, and 26, listing mottoes for chapters, and one, 25, presenting political dates drawn from the *Annual Register.* This first half of the notebook we shall speak of as *Quarry I.* The notebook was then turned over and again almost exactly half of it was used, chiefly for the working out of the structure of the novel, though a few pages are devoted to political dates concerned with the passage of the First Reform Bill. This part of the notebook we shall call *Quarry II.*

II. Other Manuscripts

Eliot, George. *Daniel Deronda.* 4 vols. British Museum Additional Manuscripts, 34,039–34,042.

————. *Felix Holt.* 3 vols. British Museum Additional Manuscripts 34,030–34,032.

————. *Middlemarch.* 4 vols. Page proof of the first (parts) edition corrected by the author. William Blackwood and Sons, Edinburgh.

————. *Middlemarch.* Page proof of the Cheap (1874) Edition corrected by the author. William Blackwood and Sons, Edinburgh.

————. *The Spanish Gypsy.* British Museum Additional Manuscripts, 34,033.

The Blackwood Papers. Correspondence between the publishers (John and William Blackwood) and George Eliot and George Henry Lewes. National Library of Scotland.

III. Printed Books and Articles

Allem, Maurice. "Notice Bibliographique," in Victor Hugo, *Les Misérables.* Paris: La Librairie Gallimarde, 1951.

Beaty, Jerome. "'Into the Irrevocable': A New George Eliot Letter," *JEGP,* 57 (October, 1958), 704-7.

————. "Visions and Revisions: Chapter lxxxi of *Middlemarch,*" PMLA, 72 (September, 1957), 662-79.

Bennett, Joan. *George Eliot: Her Mind and Her Art,* Cambridge: Cambridge University Press, 1948.

Bullett, Gerald. *George Eliot.* London: Collins, 1947.

Bulwer, Edward, Lord Lytton. "The Parisians," *Blackwood's Edinburgh Magazine,* 112-15 (October, 1872–January, 1874).

————. *The Parisians.* 4 vols. Edinburgh and London: William Blackwood and Sons [1873].

Butt, John. "The Composition of *David Copperfield* (I)," *The Dickensian,* 46 (Spring, 1950), 90-94.

Carter, John, with Michael Sadleir. *Victorian Fiction.* Cambridge: Cambridge University Press, 1947.

Cross, John W. (ed.). *George Eliot's Life as Related in Her Letters and Journals.* 3 vols. London and Edinburgh: William Blackwood and Sons, 1885.

Eliot, George. *Daniel Deronda.* 8 Books. London and Edinburgh: William Blackwood and Sons, 1876.

————. *Middlemarch.* 8 Books. London and Edinburgh: William Blackwood and Sons, 1871-72.

————. *Middlemarch.* 3 vols. Cabinet Edition. London and Edinburgh: William Blackwood and Sons [1878].

————. *The Works of George Eliot.* 21 vols. Cabinet Edition. London and Edinburgh: William Blackwood and Sons, n. d.

"George Eliot," *Blackwood's Edinburgh Magazine,* 129 (February, 1881), 255-68.

Haight, Gordon S. (ed.). *The George Eliot Letters.* 7 vols. New Haven: Yale University Press, 1954-55.

Kitchel, Anna Theresa. *George Lewes and George Eliot.* New York: The John Day Co., 1933.

Pollard, Graham. *Serial Fiction,* in *Aspects of Book Collecting.* London: Constable and Co., Ltd., 1938.

Trollope, Anthony. *The Prime Minister.* 8 Books. London: Chapman and Hall, 1875-76.

Williams, Blanche Colton. *George Eliot.* New York: The Macmillan Co., 1936.